Amy B. Middleman, MD, MSEd, MPH, Medical Editor

Kate Gruenwald Pfeifer, LCSW, Writer

This book is printed on acid-free paper.

Published by Jossey-Bass
A Wiley Imprint
One Montgomery Street, Suite 1200, San Francisco, CA 94104-4594

Developed by Nancy Hall, Inc.
Illustrations by Brie Spangler

The recommendations and information in this book are appropriate in most cases and current as of the date of publication. For more specific information about a medical condition, the AMA suggests that you consult a physician.

Readers should be aware that Internet Web sites offered as citations and/or sources for further information may have changed or disappeared between the time this was written and when it is read.

Jossey-Bass books and products are available through most bookstores. To contact Jossey-Bass directly, call our Customer Care Department within the U.S. at 800-956-7739, outside the U.S. at 317-572-3986, or fax 317-572-4002.

Jossey-Bass also publishes its books in a variety of electronic formats. Some content that appears in print may not be available in electronic books.

Library of Congress Cataloging-in-Publication Data
American Medical Association girl's guide to becoming a teen.
p. cm.
Includes index.
ISBN-13: 978-0-787-98344-4 (pbk.: alk. paper)
ISBN-10: 0-787-98344-6 (pbk.: alk. paper)
1. Puberty—Juvenile literature. 2. Teenage girls—Physiology—Juvenile literature.
I. Title: Girl's guide to becoming a teen. II. American Medical Association.
RJ144.A43 2006
613'.04243—dc22

2005034810

Printed in the United States of America

first edition

PB Printing V10005186_101118

FOREWORD

This is a very important, very exciting time in your life as you go through so many changes on your way to becoming an adult. Along with the transformation your body is undergoing, many other things in your life are changing, too. For example, your relationships with your parents and your friends may be different now than when you were younger, and people may treat you differently. Also, the way you look at things is probably not the same as it used to be. Of course, you have lots of questions. We at the American Medical Association have created this book to give you the answers to many of those questions—information that can help you grow up healthy and happy. You can also turn to your parents, your doctor, and other trusted adults whenever you need more information, guidance, or help. With more facts, you can make even better decisions to keep yourself safe.

In this book, you will learn how to deal with common concerns girls have, such as acne, menstrual cramps, and weight issues. You will learn why it's so important, even at your age, to eat a healthy diet and to be physically active. This book also discusses many of the issues that may soon be facing you or your friends, including how to resist pressure from other kids to drink alcohol, smoke cigarettes, use drugs, or start becoming sexually active.

The handy glossary at the back of the book explains some of the medical terms used in the book. Also at the end of the book, you'll find a list of helpful Web sites to go to for more information.

We at the AMA wish you good health on your journey into adulthood!

American Medical Association

AMA
AMERICAN
MEDICAL
ASSOCIATION

CONTENTS

Foreword 3

Chapter One:
Welcome to Puberty 6

Chapter Two:
Eating, Exercise, and a Healthy Weight 14

Chapter Three:
Your Height 26

Chapter Four:
Your Skin, Teeth, and Hair 32

Chapter Five:
Your Reproductive System-Inside and Out 50

Chapter Six:
Your Period 64

Chapter Seven:
Your Feelings 72

Chapter Eight:
Relationships 86

Chapter Nine:
What About Sex? 100

Find out more! 113

Glossary 116

Index 125

Chapter One:

Welcome to Puberty

Welcome to the world of the teenage girl! If you're reading this book, it's probably because you're about to be a teenager and you're curious about the changes you are starting to experience. Becoming a teenager is quite a big deal. Your body and mind are going through lots of changes—some can feel strange, some exciting, and some maybe even a little scary.

This book can help you find answers to the many questions that you and other girls your age have about puberty. Of course, it's also a good idea to talk to your parents, other family members, a doctor or nurse, or other trusted adults about any concerns you have.

Pssst! Try not to be afraid or embarrassed to ask questions. Remember, all adults were once as young as you!

What is puberty?

Puberty is the time during which your body grows from that of a child to that of an adult. Your body changes in many ways. Puberty is also the time when you will start having menstrual periods.

Changes in your body:

- You get taller.
- Your hips get wider.
- Your breasts grow.
- You grow hair in new places.
- You start having periods.

While all of these physical changes are taking place, your emotions and feelings might change too. It's not always easy to go through so many changes so quickly. Puberty can be exciting, confusing, scary, or no big deal—every girl has her own reaction, and each reaction is perfectly normal.

Does this ever happen to you?

- Your body seems to look different every week.
- Your feelings seem to change suddenly for no reason.
- You spend more time with new friends than with old ones.

How long does puberty last?

Puberty generally starts some time between the ages of 8 and 11. For some girls, it can last just a few years. For other girls, it can last 5 years or longer. Every girl is unique and will go through puberty in her own way.

How should I feel about puberty?

There is no one way you "should" feel at this time in your life. Different girls have different feelings about starting puberty. Your feelings may even change from day to day. How do you feel?

* You're excited and can't wait to start seeing the changes in your body. You are eager to feel and look more grown-up.
* You feel self-conscious about these changes and aren't quite ready yet. You may still want to be a child and don't understand why some of your friends seem in such a hurry to grow up.
* You feel both ways. Some days you're happy about growing up and other days you wish your body wasn't changing so quickly.
* You take it all in stride—and wonder what all the fuss is about.

All of these ways of feeling are normal and okay.

Why do my feelings change so much during puberty?

During puberty, most girls notice that the way they feel and think about things changes. You may become more self-conscious and concerned about how others see you. You may find that your friendships seem to be getting more complicated. You may notice that you and your parents don't agree on things as much as you used to.

It may feel like your mood can change in an instant and you don't always know why. One minute you feel like a child who wants to play, and the next minute you feel all grown-up, wanting more freedom and independence.

Does this ever happen to you?

- You're overcome by giggles that just won't let up.
- You don't know why you're crying and you can't stop.
- You're suddenly angry at someone and you don't know why.

Puberty is also a time when you may begin to think about the world and your place in it. You may start to read newspapers or watch the news, and you may become concerned about some issues in the world that worry you. You may notice something in your school or your neighborhood that troubles you. Can you make a difference, and, if so, how? These are all common thoughts and feelings that are part of being a teenager.

Some Ways You Can Make a Difference:

✲ Help an elderly neighbor.
✲ Read to a younger child.
✲ Organize a bake sale fundraiser for a worthy cause.
✲ Stop an act of bullying.
✲ When you're old enough, volunteer at a local hospital, nursing home, soup kitchen, or animal shelter.

The changes you are experiencing occur for a variety of reasons. One reason may be that your hormones are changing; *hormones* are chemicals that control many activities in your body, including growth. These changes in your hormones can also affect your mood. In addition, your way of thinking is changing as your brain further develops.

And your life is probably changing too. You may have switched schools to start middle school or junior high. You may have more pressures and responsibilities now that you are getting older. You may have made new friends, started to think about romantic relationships, or gone through a family change like divorce. These are major transformations that are likely to affect the way you feel.

If you have special needs or a long-term illness, whether or not others know about it, going through the many changes of puberty can sometimes be challenging. You're certainly not alone. Whenever you find things especially difficult, you'll feel better if you express your feelings to your parents, the doctor, the school nurse, a counselor, or another adult you trust. It can also be helpful to talk to other girls your age—you'll quickly realize that you all have a lot in common!

Why do I look at my body differently?

Girls your age often find that they start looking in the mirror more often, spend more time in the shower, and think about their appearance more than they did before.

Ideally, you like what you see when you look in the mirror. But the reality is that most girls find something, any little thing, to criticize about their appearance. It's easy to fall into the trap of comparing yourself to other girls. You may think, "I wish I weren't so tall—the short girls get all the attention" or "I'm the only girl in my gym class who doesn't wear a bra yet."

Pssst! When you don't feel you look your best, remember that everyone feels this way from time to time. It's a normal feeling because, after all, no one is perfect!

When you find yourself making these comparisons, try to remember that nobody has a perfect body, or face, or hair. Not even the fashion models you see in magazines or the stars you see in the movies. Although it's normal to find things about yourself that you want to change, it can also be harmful to be too critical of yourself. It can sometimes make you feel sad or lonely, and it can even affect your friendships.

So, try to remember the things you like about yourself and remind yourself of those things when you start to feel bad. "I may be shorter than most girls, but I'm really funny and easy to talk to." If you're having a hard time finding those good qualities in yourself, ask someone you trust—such as a good friend or an adult you look up to. You'll be surprised to hear how many wonderful things people who know you see in you.

Did you know that the photographs of women you see in most ads have been touched up quite a bit to make the women look thinner and taller and their skin smoother and unblemished? These women would look very different if you saw them in person. They would look more like everyone else—not perfect.

Stay focused on your strengths—and you'll feel good about yourself!

REAL GiRLS, REAL FEELiNGS

"When my older sister got her period, I thought she was really grown-up. Now that I have periods, it doesn't seem like such a big deal—just normal." Age 12

"It seems like all of my friends are going through puberty before me. I really want to catch up." Age 12

"When I first grew breasts, I thought they were too big and I used to wear jackets all the time to hide them. Some of my friends asked me if I stuffed my bra. I'm starting to get better about my breasts now because other girls in my class are getting bigger too." Age 13

"My breasts seem smaller than everyone else's and some kids tease me about it. Sometimes it's hard to keep from crying." Age 12

"All of a sudden, my skin is breaking out. I never had a problem before. My mom is going to take me to the skin doctor to see what I can do for it." Age 11

"I hate being the tallest girl in my class. I'm even taller than the boys!" Age 10

Chapter Two:

Eating, Exercise, and a Healthy Weight

It's especially important to be a healthy eater at this time in your life. Your brain and body need nutritious food at regular times so you can learn, grow, and be active. It's also important that you make exercise a priority in your life. The more fit you are, the better you'll look and feel. Read on to learn more about what types of food you should be eating as well as how much physical activity you should be getting.

Pssst! It's not important how skinny you can be. What's important is how healthy you can be.

Why do I need to pay attention to what I eat?

If you eat too many of the wrong kinds of foods, your body isn't getting the vitamins, minerals, and other nutrients it needs to function well and keep you healthy. Foods like french fries, chips, sugary soft drinks, and fruit drinks have lots of *calories* but few of the nutrients your body needs. Yes, fruit drinks are not so good for you because they contain a lot of sugar; it's much healthier to eat an orange or an apple or other fruit than to drink fruit juice.

How do I make sure I'm a healthy eater?

For starters, it's essential to remember to eat in moderation. This means eating sensible amounts of different kinds of foods. Of course, some foods (like fruits, vegetables, and whole-grain breads and cereals) are better for you than others (like candy bars, french fries, and sugary soft drinks). It's okay to eat a small amount of these not-so-healthy foods every now and then, but make sure you mostly eat the healthy ones.

It's also important to eat regularly, which means that you should always eat three meals a day with small, nutritious snacks in between meals. And no skipping breakfast! A healthy breakfast is especially good for you because it helps you perform better in school. Convenient, nutrient-rich snacks can be an apple or banana or another fruit, cut-up carrots or other veggies, or low-fat cheese sticks.

Does this ever happen to you?

When you skip breakfast:

- You get a headache in the middle of the morning.
- You do badly on a test.
- You fall asleep in class.
- You have trouble paying attention to the teacher.

What kinds of foods should I be eating?

Grains	Vegetables	Fruits	Milk	Meats & Beans
Eat whole-grain breads, cereals, and pastas — they're better for you than non-whole-grain foods!	Choose a colorful variety of vegetables to make sure you get a broad range of vitamins!	Grab a piece of fruit when you want a sweet snack—it has lots more nutrition than juice!	Most dairy products are high in calcium, which helps build and maintain strong bones!	Choose lean meat whenever possible. Chicken, turkey, and fish are great choices!
*Eat about 6 ounces of grains a day. Try to make at least half of them whole grains.	*Eat about $2\frac{1}{2}$ cups of vegetables a day.	*Eat about $1\frac{1}{2}$ cups of fruit a day.	*Eat about 3 cups of dairy foods a day.	*Eat about 5 ounces of meat and beans a day.

Oils: Oils from fish, nuts, and liquid oils (such as olive, soybean, or canola) are good for you in moderation!

Use this food guide pyramid to learn what types of food you should eat. You can see that you should be eating a certain number of servings of foods from each category every day, with more servings of some kinds of foods than of others. For example, you should be eating more fruits and vegetables, whole-grain breads and cereals, and low-fat dairy products like skim milk, and less sugary and fatty foods such as soft drinks, candy, cookies, and chips.

*Portion recommendations are based on an 1,800-calorie diet.

How do I make healthy decisions in the school cafeteria?

This can be tough. Although increasing numbers of schools are improving their lunch choices, many schools still serve lots of fatty fried foods and sugary snacks. But if you look around, you should be able to find some good choices. Look for salads, soups, and fruits, as well as sandwiches and wraps (but watch out for high-fat dressings and toppings). Avoid sugary soft drinks, fruit drinks, cookies, and cakes. For drinks, choose water or low-fat milk. An occasional non-sugar diet soft drink is okay.

Is it okay for teenagers to be vegetarians?

Vegetarians need to focus even more than other people on eating a balanced diet. Restricting whole food groups from your diet can be harmful to your health, especially at your age. If you eliminate meat and poultry from your diet, you need to add other *protein* sources because protein is essential for your body to grow properly. Good non-meat protein sources include kidney beans and other beans, eggs, low-fat milk and cheese, nuts, and tofu.

Because of your age and the importance of getting enough *nutrients* to grow and develop properly, you should talk to your doctor before you make any changes in your eating habits. The doctor may recommend that you meet with a *dietitian*; a dietitian is a health professional who teaches people how to eat healthfully. The dietitian can tell you about different food combinations you should eat to make sure you are getting the right amounts of *vitamins, minerals,* and other nutrients to stay healthy. But just to be safe, it's a good idea to also take a daily multivitamin/mineral supplement.

There are so many ways besides playing team sports to be active!

- Go for a hike.
- Ride a bike.
- Do jumping jacks.
- Dance to music.
- Swim some laps.
- Do some push-ups.
- Go for a run.
- Strike a yoga pose.
- Pull weeds in a garden.
- Walk the dog.
- Play tennis with friends.
- Follow a pilates video.
- Vacuum your room.
- Jump rope.
- Kick a ball.
- Do some pull-ups.
- Cartwheel across a yard.
- Go in-line skating.
- Ski down a slope.
- Shoot some baskets.

Why is exercise so important?

Regular exercise is just as important to good health as eating a nutritious diet. Exercise makes you fit, keeps your heart and lungs healthy, strengthens your muscles and bones, and helps you reach or stay at a healthy weight. Exercise also makes you feel good because it can relieve stress, boost your mood, and improve your self-esteem.

Strengthening exercise builds muscle by forcing the muscles to work against the weight of your body or an object such as a weight. Strengthening exercise is also good for your heart and it keeps you fit.

Aerobic exercise includes any activity that uses the large muscles, such as those in the legs, in repetitive motion. Aerobic exercise makes the heart and lungs work more efficiently, builds endurance, reduces body fat, and builds muscle.

Flexibility exercise such as doing stretches improves the movement of your muscles and joints. Being flexible increases your ability to perform everyday activities and protects your muscles from injury.

Exercise not only keeps you healthy—it makes you look and feel good!

How much do I need to exercise?

It's essential to be physically active every day—for 1 hour at the very least. For some girls, this means playing on a sports team. If you aren't interested in team sports, find other ways to be active. An easy way to get more exercise is to fit more activity into your everyday routine. Instead of getting a ride to school or the mall, walk or ride your bike if you can (as long as your parents think it's safe), go jogging or for long walks with friends, take the stairs instead of the elevator, or walk the dog. At home, you can jump rope, follow an exercise video, or use a treadmill or stationary bike. Include push-ups, sit-ups, and other strengthening exercises in your exercise routine.

While anything that gets you moving is good, more *vigorous* activities that make your heart beat faster give you even more health benefits. What's important is to find something you love doing. But if you have any health problems or concerns, check with your doctor before starting an exercise program.

Will my weight change during puberty?

You will notice during puberty that the shape of your body changes. You will develop breasts, your hips will get wider, and your body will become curvier. You need to gain weight in order for these changes to occur. Many girls at this age worry about becoming overweight, but remember that it is normal to gain weight more quickly during these years.

Your weight depends on your body type as well as on *heredity*. Whatever type of body people in your family tend to have—tall, short, narrow, or curvy—chances are that your body will be a similar shape and size. But, of course, your weight also depends quite a lot on how much you eat and how active you are.

If your doctor has told you that you are overweight for your age and height, you can help yourself by learning more about how to make healthy food choices and how to be more physically active than you have been. Because you will naturally gain more weight during puberty, this is a good time to begin changing your eating and exercise habits.

Why do so many girls worry about their weight?

Your body doesn't look like anyone else's. You may compare your body to that of other girls in your class—or to girls and women you see on television, in movies, and in magazines. You may be concerned that you aren't as thin, or as muscular, or as curvy as other girls.

Worrying a lot about your body and weight can affect the way you feel about yourself. Some girls say that whenever they're feeling bad about how they look, it helps to remember the things they like about themselves, such as their ability to play the piano, be a winning soccer goalie, or write creative stories. When you find yourself constantly thinking about your weight or your body, it's important to talk to a trusted grown-up who can help you focus on the more important qualities.

What should I do if I think I need to lose weight?

First, talk to your mom or dad, and then talk to your doctor. Many girls think they're overweight when they aren't, so it's important to have an evaluation by the doctor. If, after examining you and checking your weight and height, the doctor tells you that you are overweight for your age and height, he or she will suggest steps you can take to lose those extra pounds. Or the strategy may be to help you keep from gaining more weight and then, as you get taller, you will "grow into" your weight.

The first step the doctor may recommend is to become more physically active than you have been. The more active you are, the more calories your body burns. If you have been inactive for a long time, your doctor will suggest gradually, little by little, working up to more strenuous activities.

Your goal should be to get at least 1 hour of physical activity every day. Your effort to reach a healthy weight is more likely to be successful if you also cut back on watching TV, surfing the Internet, and playing video games to no more than 1 hour a day. (These activities also keep you from more important things like homework, and too much time on the Internet can put you at risk of coming into contact with inappropriate chat rooms or people who could harm you.)

Of course, eating more of the nutritious foods such as fruits and vegetables, which tend to be low in calories, and less of the high-calorie, non-nutritious foods such as sugary soft drinks and fast foods will also help you stay fit and avoid health problems.

These changes are very hard to make for anyone, at any age, but especially for someone as young as you. To make it easier for yourself, get your parents and other family members involved with you.

Keep in mind that it is not healthy to lose weight quickly. Weight-loss diets that strictly limit the amount and types of foods you eat can be especially harmful for people your age. If you don't eat enough, your body may not get the nourishment it needs for you to grow and develop and go through the normal changes of puberty. Girls who lose weight too quickly or lose too much weight may stop having periods or delay starting their periods and have other health problems such as bone loss. This is the time to see the doctor.

What if I think I'm too thin?

Some girls worry about being skinny. If you are one of those girls, share your concerns with your family and your doctor. You may be thin because you have begun your growth spurt and gotten taller but haven't started your weight spurt yet. Or you may be in a family that naturally tends to be very thin.

If you want to gain some weight and the doctor thinks it's okay for you to do so, you might try eating more often, by adding an additional healthy snack or two between meals. Whatever you do, don't eat fatty or sugary junk foods as a way to gain weight, because too much fat and sugar can be harmful.

What are eating disorders?

Most people eat to get energy and to feel good. For some people, more often girls than boys, eating behaviors and feelings about food can become negative. They may think about food all the time, measure everything they eat, hide their eating from people, and worry excessively about their weight and body shape. They often have a distorted body image—they think they're fat when, in reality, they're extremely thin.

These negative thoughts and eating behaviors can be dangerous. They can harm your body permanently and some can even be fatal.

Eating Disorders

* ***Anorexia nervosa*** When someone doesn't eat enough and becomes dangerously thin.
* ***Bulimia nervosa*** When someone eats a very large amount of food very quickly (binges) and then eliminates the food or calories (purges) by vomiting or taking laxatives or compensating for it by exercising excessively or strictly cutting back on eating after the binge.
* ***Compulsive overeating*** When someone eats large amounts of food, usually not because of hunger but because of stress or strong emotions like sadness.

What if I notice that a friend has a problem with eating?

If you are worried about a friend's eating behavior, it's important to tell an adult as soon as possible. This type of problem is usually too complicated for a young person to handle alone. Talk to one of your parents, a favorite aunt, a trusted teacher or guidance counselor, or the school nurse. They can make sure your friend gets the help she needs. If your friend does have a serious eating problem, her health and even her life could be in danger.

You may worry that you are betraying your friend by sharing this concern. But in reality, you are being the best kind of friend. You want to make sure your friend is safe and healthy.

REAL GiRLS, REAL FEELiNGS

"Sometimes when I look in the mirror I feel ugly. Other days I look in the mirror and I like what I see. It can be confusing!" Age 11

"Even though I'm overweight, I want to be an actress someday. Some people tease me because they say actresses are supposed to be skinny. I try not to let it bother me." Age 12

"Whenever I sit down I look at my thighs and think they're fat. I always bring a sweater to cover them up." Age 11

"Recently I decided to become a vegetarian. At first my parents didn't want me to. Then I told them my reasons why, and they said it was okay. I had to talk to my doctor about how to be a healthy vegetarian. Sometimes it's hard work, but I'm glad I stuck with my decision." Age 13

"I'm a little overweight. I tried to go on a diet, but my mom told me that cutting out too much food isn't good for someone my age. Now I'm exercising more and hoping that will help." Age 11

"I feel good about my body. I play a lot of sports and know that I'm strong. I especially like that my legs are muscular." Age 12

"I'm naturally skinny. I eat a lot, but I just don't put on weight. It's really annoying because I feel like I look younger than everyone else." Age 10

Chapter Three:
Your Height

One change that your body goes through during puberty is something that you are already used to—growing taller. The difference now is that you are growing at a much faster rate. This is called a growth spurt. When you were younger, you probably grew just a couple of inches each year. During puberty, you may grow as much as 4 inches or more in a year!

When will I experience my growth spurt?

For most girls, this occurs toward the beginning of puberty, while, for most boys, it occurs later in puberty. This is why so many girls in middle school are taller than the boys.

What if I feel too tall or too short?

Just like every other part of puberty, you will go through your growth spurt in your own time and at your own pace. You may go through it earlier or later than other girls your age. You may find yourself, at least temporarily, the tallest person in your grade—or the shortest. Sometimes the girls who have early growth spurts stop their spurt before other girls and don't always end up being the tallest as adults.

{ **Pssst!** Did you know that your feet will grow longer before you begin to get taller? You may feel awkward for a time, but don't worry, things will soon balance out again. }

Do you ever feel this way?

"I'm one of the tallest kids in my grade, even taller than almost every boy. Some of the kids like to tease me. I wish I were shorter—it would be so much easier to fit in."

"I'm tired of being so short when everyone else seems to be getting taller. When will I grow? People don't believe me when I say I'm in middle school, and some kids joke that I look like a 3rd grader."

Unless you are the average height, you may feel uncomfortable at times. It's important to remember that your height has nothing to do with who you are as a person. Instead of focusing on your height—which you can't change—focus on other, more important qualities. Concentrate on what makes you feel good about yourself, like your sense of humor, your ability to play the flute, or your skills as an athlete.

When will I stop growing?

Your growth spurt will start to slow down around the time you get your first menstrual period. After that, most girls continue to grow—but at a slower pace—for another 1 to 3 years.

How tall will I be?

No one can predict your exact future height. For the most part, your height depends on heredity, which means it is generally based on how tall most people in your family are. For example, if most of your family members are on the short side, it is likely that you will be on the shorter side, too. Of course, height also depends on eating a healthy diet.

For fun, try the following formula to get an estimate of how tall you might be. First, find out the height in inches of both of your parents. (Don't forget that you have to multiply the number of feet by 12 to turn feet into inches; so if your dad is 6 feet tall, he is 6 x 12 = 72 inches tall.) Then subtract 5 inches from your dad's height and add this number to your mom's height. Divide the sum by 2. Although there is no way to precisely predict a person's future height, this formula can give you a measurement to think about. After all, it is possible that you might end up being much taller or much shorter than both of your parents—or anyone else in your family!

Formula for estimating your height

1. Write down your dad's height (in inches)
2. Subtract 5
3. Add your mom's height (in inches)
4. Divide the total number by 2

Get Your Calcium!

Some types of juice, cereal, and bread have calcium added to them. Other foods—like the 10 listed below—are naturally high in calcium.

But remember to choose the low-fat or fat-free versions of dairy products!

- milk
- cheese
- yogurt
- baked beans
- broccoli
- dried figs
- tofu
- almonds
- pudding
- salmon

Why does my doctor tell me that I need calcium?

Calcium is an important mineral that your body needs to help keep your bones and teeth strong. This is the crucial time for building your bones, because they gain the most strength during the teen years. The stronger your bones are now, the stronger they will be throughout your life and the less likely that you will have problems.

You can find calcium in dairy foods such as low-fat milk, cheese, and yogurt. Low-fat and fat-free milk have just as much calcium in a glass as full-fat or 2-percent milk. If you don't or can't drink milk, drink lactose-free milk and eat non-dairy foods that have calcium naturally or that have added calcium. Non-dairy foods that are naturally rich in calcium include navy beans and other beans, canned salmon, kale and other greens, and broccoli. Calcium is added to many foods such as orange juice, soy milk, and many breads and cereals. The label on the food package will tell you if it's calcium-fortified.

Don't forget that this is the best time in your life to build up your bones!

Why does my doctor test me for scoliosis? What is scoliosis?

Scoliosis is a condition in which a person's spine curves to the left or right. Most kids learn that they have scoliosis while they are going through their growth spurt—usually between the ages of 10 and 16. Scoliosis is more common in girls than in boys. If the curve is mild, it doesn't require any treatment. If the curve is significant, the doctor may recommend special exercises to help straighten it. Sometimes surgery or other treatment is necessary to correct the curve.

Chapter Four:

Your Skin, Teeth, and Hair

You probably didn't pay a lot of attention to your skin when you were younger. Your parents told you when to bathe or shower, and they were always reminding you to wash your hands. Now that you are older, you are ready to take responsibility for this part of your self-care routine.

Many girls notice during puberty that their skin feels and looks more oily than before. This is because an increase in hormones in your body during this time causes your skin to produce more oil. This particular oily substance, which *lubricates* the skin, is called *sebum.*

Psssst! Pimples are not caused by any foods you eat—not even chocolate or greasy foods. They're not caused by dirt, either.

What causes pimples?

Pimples are *blemishes* that can result when the skin produces an oily substance (sebum) that gets trapped under the skin in the *hair follicles*. (Follicles are the openings in your skin through which hair grows.) When sebum gets trapped in a hair follicle, it produces a blemish called a *blackhead* or *whitehead*. Then, if *bacteria* get into the blocked follicle and multiply, they can cause a reaction (which doctors call *inflammation*) that creates a pimple. (Bacteria are always on your skin and usually cause no problems.)

Pimples are red lumps on the skin that are filled with a substance called *pus*; pus is produced when your body tries to fight the bacteria inside the follicle. If you have blackheads, whiteheads, or pimples, the condition is called *acne*. Sometimes, taking certain kinds of medications, such as *steroids*, can cause acne. If you have acne after you start taking a medication, talk to your doctor.

Although pimples usually appear on the face, they can also develop on the neck, back, chest, buttocks, and, sometimes, the upper arms and thighs. Acne usually clears up in the late teens, although some people get it later in life.

Did you know that pimples don't just affect pre-teens and teens? Some adults get acne, too.

What, exactly, are blackheads and whiteheads?

Blackheads, which look black on the surface of the skin, are blockages in hair follicles that have turned dark because they're exposed to oxygen in the air. Whiteheads, which look white on the surface of the skin, are follicles that are filled with the same material as blackheads but they have only a tiny opening in the skin. Whiteheads are white because the air cannot reach them through this tiny opening. If the oil inside the hair follicle can't get out and it builds up along with the bacteria, the blackhead or whitehead can turn into a pimple.

Why do some girls get more pimples than others?

As with every other aspect of puberty, each girl's skin reacts differently to the hormone changes of puberty. Your hormones may cause your body to produce more oil or less oil than another girl's. You may discover that members of your family, including your mom and dad, had lots of pimples when they were teenagers. Acne can run in families.

What makes pimples worse?

Leave that pimple alone and it will go away faster!

The worst thing you can do to a pimple is to pick it. If you squeeze, poke, or push at a pimple, it will irritate it even more. Also, if you scrub or scrape your face too much when you wash it, you can irritate blemishes and make them worse.

If you have a tendency to get pimples, use only makeup and hair products that are "oil-free" or "non-comedogenic." (*Non-comedogenic* means that it does not clog pores.) Check labels for these terms. If your skin breaks out after using a certain product, stop using it. If you have acne just around your hairline, consider changing hair products. Ask your doctor what products you can use that will be less likely to cause blemishes.

Stress and nervousness can make pimples worse. You may notice that you get more pimples before a big test at school or other stress or at certain times of the month, like around the time of your period. Both stress and the menstrual cycle cause changes in hormones, which can increase oil production in the skin.

How can I clear up my pimples?

Wash your face twice a day with a mild, unscented soap or cleanser. Don't use moisturizers unless absolutely necessary to keep your skin from getting too dry; if you feel you need to use a moisturizer, ask your doctor to recommend one.

If you wear foundation makeup, use only a water-based one that is non-comedogenic and always remove it completely.

You can find many products at the drugstore that can help with pimples. Look for products that contain *benzoyl peroxide*; ask your doctor to recommend one. He or she may suggest starting with a lower strength of the product and working up to a higher strength if the lower strength doesn't work.

Generally, you apply these products to your skin once or twice a day. If your skin becomes red or irritated, try using the product every other day or every third day. But be careful using benzoyl peroxide because it can stain your clothes.

If, after a few weeks of using the product, your skin doesn't get better, see your doctor. He or she may suggest an over-the-counter product that contains *salicylic acid,* which can be very helpful for skin that is acne-prone. Or your doctor may give you a prescription for a different acne medication, or prescribe an *antibiotic* (a type of medicine that treats infections caused by bacteria) to help with your skin. If the usual medications don't work, the doctor may recommend that you see a dermatologist. A *dermatologist* is a doctor who treats skin problems.

- Keep your skin clean and moisturized.
- Once you start puberty, try to shower or bathe every day.
- Use a moisturizing lotion on your skin after bathing or showering to help keep your skin from getting too dry.
- If your skin tends to be oily, use a non-oily, non-comedogenic moisturizer.

What else do I need to do to take care of my skin?

It's also important to protect your skin from the sun. You may think that getting a tan makes you look healthy but, in fact, a sunburn or tan is a sign of skin damage—that's how your skin protects itself. Too much sun is the major cause of wrinkles and skin cancer. (Smoking is the second leading cause of wrinkles, and it also makes your skin and teeth yellow!) To protect your skin, use sunscreen whenever you're outside. If you use makeup or moisturizer, consider those that have built-in *sun protection factor* (*SPF*). (You should also wear sunglasses that provide UV—ultraviolet—protection for your eyes.)

Always avoid tanning salons! Tanning beds are just as harmful to your skin as the sun. If you really want the look of a tan, a safer alternative is to use a sunless tanning product. These come in sprays and lotions and many contain SPF. Some salons also provide sunless tanning methods such as sprays.

SUNSCREEN 4-1-1

There are many types of sunscreen to choose from. The brand you choose is not important but the SPF is. SPF, which stands for sun protection factor, is listed on the product label. The lowest, least-protective SPF you can find is 2; the highest is 50. Use a sunscreen with an SPF of at least 15 every time you plan to be outside. If you are very fair or tend to burn, use an SPF of 30 or higher.

What if I notice other changes in my skin?

You may notice other skin conditions besides acne as you begin puberty. If you notice anything new or unusual, make sure you tell your parents and see your doctor. The doctor can identify the condition and tell you how best to treat it.

Some common skin conditions

- ***Warts*** Hard lumps with a rough surface that are caused by a virus. (Viruses are germs that can cause different kinds of infections, including the common cold.) Warts often develop on the arms, legs, hands, and face. Some types of warts, called plantar warts, occur on the bottoms of the feet.
- ***Moles*** Round or oval spots on the skin that are usually dark brown. Some moles are flat and some can be raised. If your moles change, tell your parents, who may want to have the doctor check them.
- ***Eczema*** Red, itchy patches on the skin that sometimes join together. The skin can become dry and lighter or darker than the surrounding skin, and, after too much scratching, may look like leather. Eczema often occurs on the inner part of the elbows or behind the knees.
- ***Psoriasis*** Patches of thick, raised skin that are pink or red and covered with silverish white scales. It can occasionally cause mild itching or soreness. Psoriasis most often occurs on the knees, elbows, and scalp.
- ***Acanthosis Nigricans*** Raised, velvety darkened patches on the back of the neck, armpits, and groin that make the skin look dirty. Occurs most often in young people who are overweight, and it is strongly linked to type 2 diabetes. Losing weight helps the patches fade. It should be evaluated by a doctor.

What are stretch marks?

When a person grows quickly, purple or white lines can appear on the skin. The rapid growth can cause the skin to stretch, which is why these lines are called *stretch marks*. The most common places to find stretch marks are the thighs, buttocks, and breasts. Stretch marks usually fade over time.

Why do I have body odor all of a sudden? What can I do about it?

Your body will begin to sweat more in some places during puberty. One area you will notice this is under your arms. You have *glands* under your arms that attract bacteria. These bacteria, when combined with sweat, can cause an odor.

Body odor is a normal part of puberty but, of course, it can be embarrassing. Nobody wants to be told they smell bad. Fortunately, there are some easy ways to prevent and eliminate body odor.

One way to help prevent or reduce body odor is to bathe or shower every day, and wear clean clothes every day. (This may be a good time to start doing your own laundry!)

Deodorants and Antiperspirants

Deodorants are used to prevent body odor, while *antiperspirants* reduce sweating. However, some deodorants are also antiperspirants and perform both functions. The product labels tell you what they are.

Using a deodorant or an antiperspirant can also help prevent or reduce body odor. These products come in different forms. Some deodorants can be sprayed on, some come in liquids that are rolled on, and some come in a gel or stick. If you have a skin reaction like a rash after using one of these products, it could be because it contains aluminum. Some people are allergic to aluminum. Try a product that does not contain aluminum.

Lately, my feet sometimes smell bad. What can I do?

Like body odor, foot odor can be embarrassing. One way to avoid foot odor, or to keep it to a minimum, is to keep your feet as clean as possible at all times. Also, wear cotton socks, which can absorb sweat from your feet. Avoid shoes that are made of plastic, rubber, or other man-made materials. These materials don't allow air to reach your feet, causing your feet to sweat and, possibly, smell.

If your shoes smell, you can buy an over-the-counter foot powder or odor-controlling shoe insert. These products target foot odor by absorbing sweat. They are available at most drugstores, are easy to use, and are generally inexpensive. If your feet continue to smell bad, talk to your doctor; you could have an infection called athlete's foot.

Pssst! Make sure you talk to your parents before you make a decision about getting a piercing or tattoo.

Are body piercings and tattoos safe?

Getting your ears pierced is usually very safe—as long as it is done by an experienced professional using *sterile* equipment. Do not pierce your ears yourself or have a friend do it. The best option is to find a doctor who will pierce your ears.

Even when done by a healthcare professional, any kind of piercing carries the risk of *infection*. So it's very important to carefully follow the post-piercing instructions to avoid infection and help the piercing heal properly.

Piercings in other parts of the body, such as the navel, are more likely to result in infections and they can also be more painful and take a longer time to heal than the ears. Getting your tongue pierced may be trendy, but you run the risk of an infection and swelling that could make eating, speaking, and even breathing difficult. A tongue piercing can also cause nerve damage, gum disease, loss of taste, and chipped teeth.

Tattoos also carry the risk of infection. Unlike piercings, tattoos are permanent. It's very difficult—and expensive—to have a tattoo removed, and it can leave scars. You may like the idea and look of a tattoo now, but that doesn't mean you always will. Seriously think about these issues before getting a tattoo. If you tend to form thick scars (*keloids*), you may not want to pierce or mark your skin in any way. Why not experiment with temporary tattoos? They're much safer and a great way to express yourself. You can be creative and change your art whenever you get tired of a tattoo!

Most states regulate places that provide tattoos and piercings to ensure that they are safe. It is against the law in most states to provide a tattoo to anyone under age 18 without the consent of a parent. Many states make it illegal to provide a body piercing to anyone under 18 even with a parent's consent. You do NOT want to get a tattoo or body piercing from a place that is not regulated—it's unsafe and against the law.

Why do I have to brush and floss my teeth every day?

You may not realize it now, but healthy teeth and gums are an important part of staying healthy. If you allow bacteria and other germs to grow in your teeth and gums, your teeth can decay and you could lose them. These germs can also make your gums bleed and your breath smell bad.

But most harmful to your health, the bacteria in your mouth can go into other parts of your body and cause serious problems, even with your heart. That's why your parents are always reminding you to brush your teeth every morning and night, and sometimes more often (like if you have braces). Listen to your parents—and see the dentist every 6 months for a checkup and cleaning to make sure your teeth and gums stay healthy.

Is there anything I can do to make my teeth whiter?

If you want to whiten your teeth, talk to your dentist about it. Most dentists can provide bleaching kits that people can use at home. Your dentist may recommend whitening strips that you can buy in a drugstore. These strips are coated with a thick solution of *hydrogen peroxide*. You apply the strips once or twice a day for half an hour for a certain number of days or weeks. The strips can sometimes cause gum irritation but are generally considered safe. Be sure you talk to your parents and dentist first.

Why do I suddenly care so much about my hair?

It's normal for girls who are beginning puberty to become more self-conscious. You may think and worry much more about yourself than you did before. In addition to worrying about your height, weight, and skin, you may begin to worry about your hair.

Your hair is one of the many things that can make you stand out from other girls. Long, short, curly, or straight—all types of hair can be beautiful. Many girls with straight hair wish they had curls, and those with curly hair often wish for smooth, straight hair.

Of course, you can work to change your hair's natural look—by using a blow dryer, flat iron or curling iron, or by getting a chemical treatment like a perm. But accepting your hair as it is naturally can boost your self-confidence and make you feel better about yourself.

Hair is another thing about you that is hereditary (the passing on of qualities and traits from one generation to the next.) Your hair is probably like someone else's in your family. If it is, ask a family member with similar hair for ideas on how to best manage and style it.

Is it okay to color my hair? How can I do it?

Many girls wonder what they would look like with their hair a different color. Some girls with dark hair wish it were lighter, while girls with light hair wish it were darker. Some girls are even attracted to hair colors that aren't possible in nature, like pink or blue!

Ideally, you're happy with yourself as you are. But if you're eager to change your hair color, be sure to talk with your parents first. If they give you permission, you have a couple of options. You can have a professional stylist color your hair in a salon. If you choose to do this, bring along some pictures of the color you have in mind. Or you can color your hair yourself with an over-the-counter product from a drugstore. But be careful—the color may end up looking different from the way it looks on the package. For example, some girls who want to add a little red to their hair can end up with purple hair!

Don't forget, though, that your hair will grow back in your natural color; the more contrast there is between your treated hair color and your natural hair color, the more noticeable your roots will be when your hair grows in. If you want to keep your hair a different color, you will need to continue having it dyed or bleached. Also keep in mind that having your hair colored at a salon can be expensive.

> **Pssst!** Remember that you have options besides coloring your hair should you want a new look—even a simple haircut might do the trick!

Most important, be aware that hair dyes and bleaches are made of chemicals—and chemicals can damage the hair. So, ask yourself before you change your hair color: Is it worth the risk of damage to your hair just to change its color?

Why is hair growing in new places on my body?

Growing hair in new places on your body is another change to your body during puberty. Hair will begin to grow under your arms, and you will start noticing hair in your *genital* area. Hair that grows in the genital area is called *pubic hair*. Pubic hair is usually coarser and darker than the hair on your head, legs, or arms, and it's usually curlier than your other hair. You may also notice that the hair on your arms or legs is getting darker or thicker. Some girls grow hair above their upper lip.

These are all normal places for hair to grow during puberty. However, if you notice that you are growing hair on your chest or your chin, you need to see your doctor. Hair growing in these places can be a sign of a possible hormone imbalance.

When will I start getting pubic hair?

You will probably start getting pubic hair at the beginning of puberty. Of course—just like everything else that occurs during puberty—it can happen at any time. Some girls grow pubic hair earlier or later than other girls.

{ **Pssst!** Remember that the five stages on the next page won't necessarily match up to your stage of breast development. You can be in stage four of breast development, but be in stage two of pubic hair growth. }

The five stages of pubic hair growth

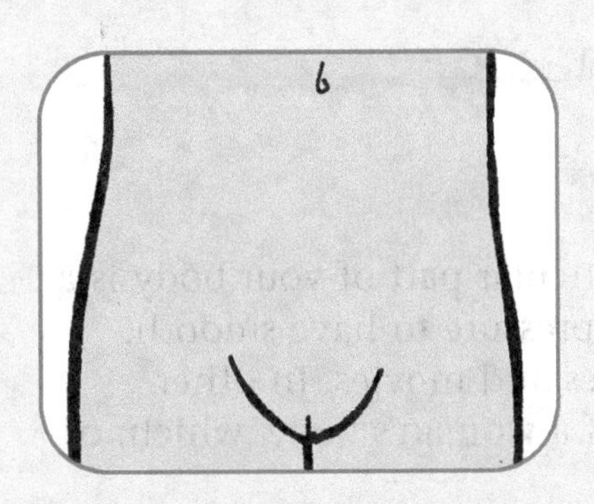

Stage 1: You do not have any pubic hair yet.

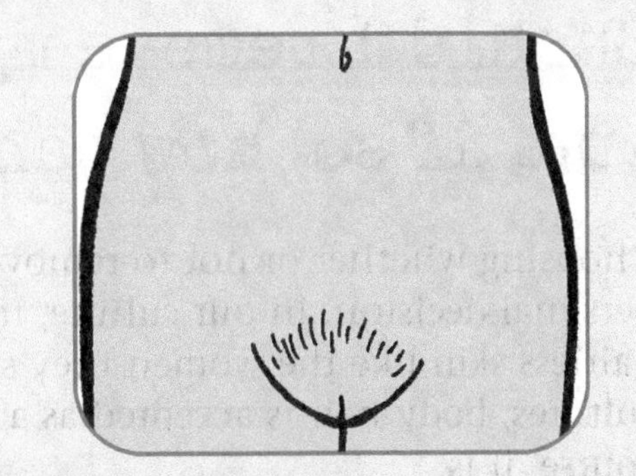

Stage 2: You begin to see a few pubic hairs, which are straight.

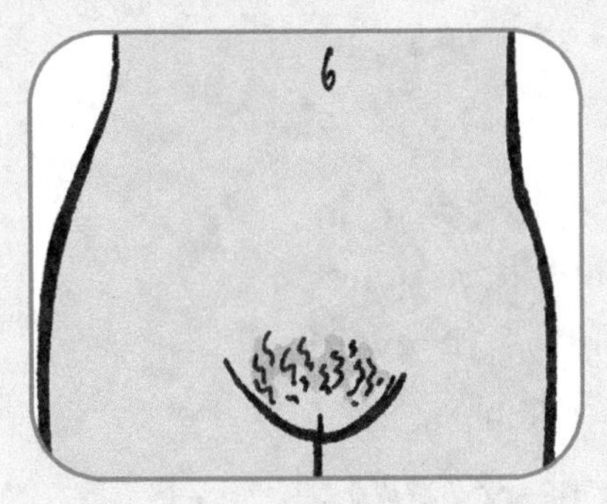

Stage 3: Your pubic hair becomes curlier and darker.

Stage 4: The hair grows over the pubic bone and usually becomes thicker and coarser and begins to form a triangle shape.

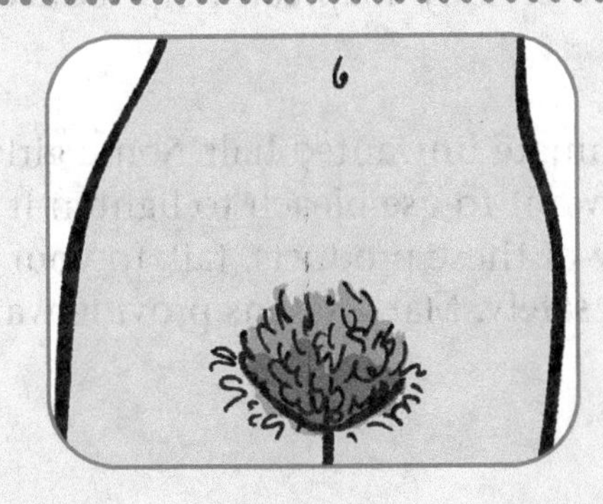

Stage 5: Your pubic hair forms a thicker triangle and grows out onto the inner thighs.

Should I remove my body hair and, if so, how can I do it?

Choosing whether or not to remove hair in a particular part of your body is a personal decision. In our culture, many girls feel pressure to have smooth, hairless skin like the women they see in magazines and movies. In other cultures, body hair is accepted as a natural part of a woman's body, which, of course, it is.

If you decide that you want to remove your body hair, you have a number of choices. You may decide to shave the hair on your legs and under your arms. You may also choose to shave the "bikini" area on your upper thighs where pubic hair can grow. Electric razors work well and are safer than non-electric razors because they're less likely to cause cuts.

Be sure to shave in the direction your hair grows to avoid "shaving bumps," also known as *folliculitis*, especially on areas of sensitive skin.

There are two types of disposable razors. One kind can be used a few times and then the entire razor is thrown away. Another kind has a disposable razor head that needs to be replaced after a few uses. Disposable razors generally work well. Some, however, can cause cuts and an itchy rash. Using shaving cream or a creamy soap can help reduce these problems.

You can also use hair removal cream to eliminate unwanted hair. Some girls who have dark hair on their upper lip may want to use bleach to lighten it instead of removing it. But before using any of these products, talk to your parents. They can help you use the product safely. Many salons provide waxing techniques to remove unwanted hair. Hair takes longer to grow back after waxing. Some girls and women have hair in certain parts of their body removed permanently with procedures such as laser hair removal and *electrolysis*. These procedures are done by trained, licensed professionals and can be expensive.

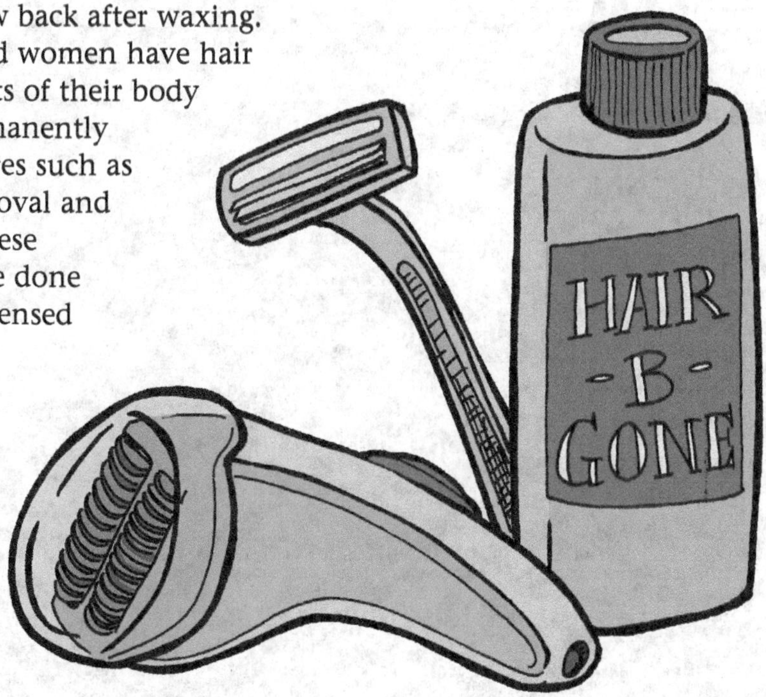

MYTHBUSTER

Shaving will not make your hair grow back thicker or coarser. When it first begins to grow back, you will notice that the hairs are very short and coarse. If you allow the hair to grow out, you'll see that it becomes as soft as your other hair.

Chapter Five:

Your Reproductive System—Inside and Out

Probably the most significant changes that occur during puberty are with your reproductive system. Some of these changes are not so easy to notice because part of your reproductive system is inside your body. Other changes, such as the development of breasts, are easy to see. You may feel proud and excited about developing breasts, or you may feel self-conscious about it. Both of these feelings are normal. Some girls develop earlier or later than others. Remember that, like every other transformation that occurs during puberty, each girl goes through these changes at her own pace.

What are breasts made of?

The major function of the breasts is to produce milk for a baby. Your breasts are made up mostly of fat. They are also made up of milk glands and milk ducts. When you have a baby, the milk glands produce milk and the milk ducts carry the milk from the glands to the *nipples* to provide milk for the baby. You have muscles under your breasts and in the chest wall, but you do not have muscles you can build up inside your breasts. That's why no amount of exercise will make your breasts bigger.

What determines the size of my breasts?

Your breast size is based mostly on heredity. If the women in your family tend to have large breasts, then you are likely to as well. Weight can also have an impact on breast size—gaining weight often makes the breasts bigger.

Breasts can start to develop on girls as young as 8 and can continue to change even into a woman's early twenties!

How long will it take for my breasts to grow?

Generally, breasts grow in five stages. Many girls go through these stages in the order shown on the next page. But some girls may skip a stage, which is normal for them. You may go through these stages quickly, in just a couple of years. Or you may take longer—some girls' breasts don't reach full size and shape until they become pregnant. Each girl's experience is unique, as are her breasts.

The five stages of breast development

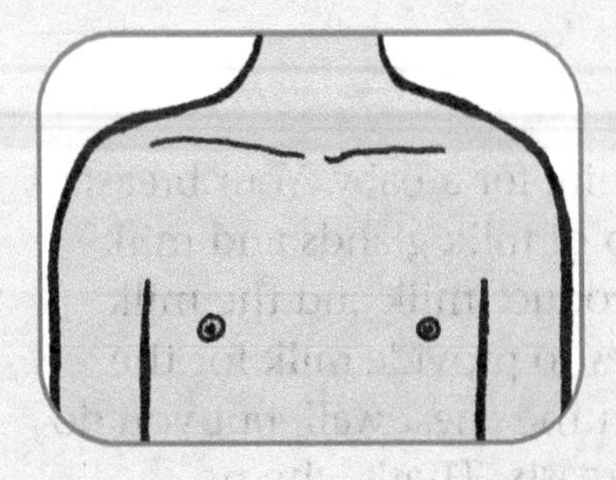

STAGE 1: Your chest still looks like it did when you were younger. Your nipples stick out a little, but otherwise your chest is basically flat.

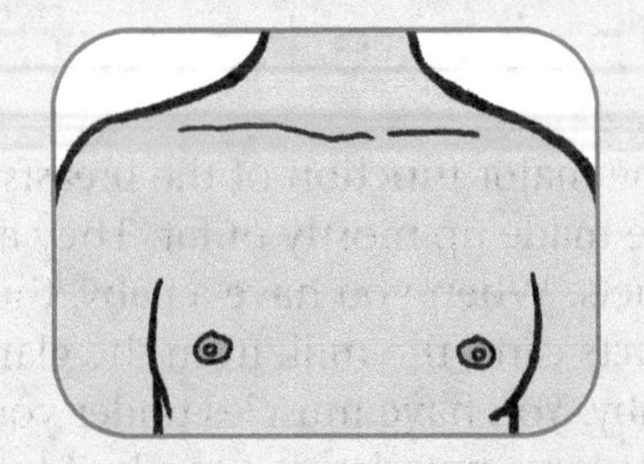

STAGE 2: This stage usually begins sometime between the ages of 8 and 12. During this stage you develop *breast buds*, lumps of tissue that develop under your nipples. These lumps are the first sign that your breasts are beginning to grow. They may feel sore at first, which is normal. If you have not started this stage by the time you're 13, you should see your doctor for a checkup.

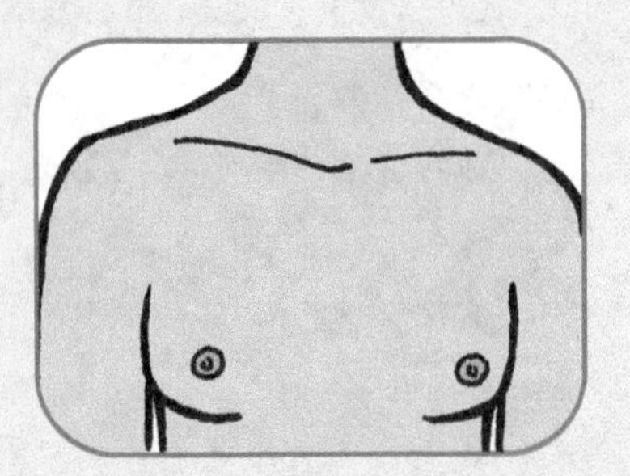

STAGE 3: Your breasts continue to grow during this stage. Your nipples may get larger and darker in color. You may consider wearing a bra at this point, if you're not already wearing one.

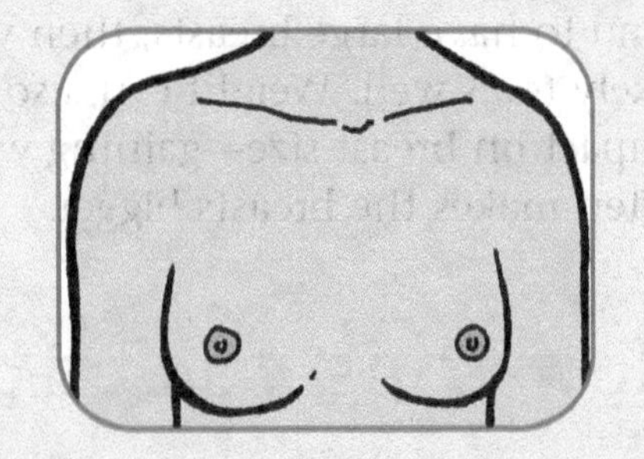

STAGE 4: During this stage, your nipples will seem to form a separate mound on your breasts, while at the same time continuing to grow bigger. Some girls seem to skip this stage.

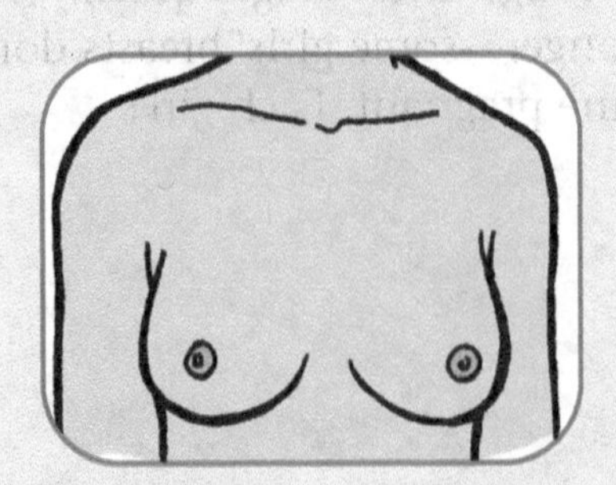

STAGE 5: This is the last stage of breast development. Your breasts have probably reached their final size.

What if I'm not happy with how my breasts look?

No one has perfect breasts. Every girl's breasts are unique. It's best to accept your breasts the way they are, even if you think they are too small or too big or you don't like the shape. Keep in mind that the size and shape of your breasts have nothing to do with their function. This means that breast size and shape do not determine whether you will be able to breastfeed a baby if you choose to. There are no creams or other products that will increase or decrease the size of your breasts. If you find yourself worrying a lot about your breast size, share your worries with a trusted adult. In order to feel good about yourself, you need to learn to accept all parts of yourself.

My breasts are not the same size. Is that normal?

Many girls worry about their breasts being different sizes. This is not unusual. For some girls, one breast develops at a faster rate than the other. The slower-developing breast will usually catch up. However, it's possible that it won't and the breasts will be shaped or sized slightly differently.

These differences usually aren't very noticeable. But sometimes they are. It should not be cause for concern. If you feel that your breasts are obviously unequal, keep in mind that it is probably much more noticeable to you than it is to anyone else. Chances are that if you don't pay any attention to it, nobody else will notice it either! But if it bothers you, you may want to use a bra insert on the smaller side during the time that breast is catching up with the other one.

Why am I getting white lines on my breasts?

Stretch marks, which usually look like white or purple lines on the skin, may appear on your breasts if they are growing quickly. Stretch marks develop when rapid growth causes the skin to stretch. Stretch marks usually fade over time.

What will happen to my nipples during puberty?

Your nipples will become larger and often darker in color during puberty. You may begin to notice that each nipple has two parts. The actual nipple is the raised bump in the middle of your breast. The *areola* is the darker-colored circle of skin surrounding it.

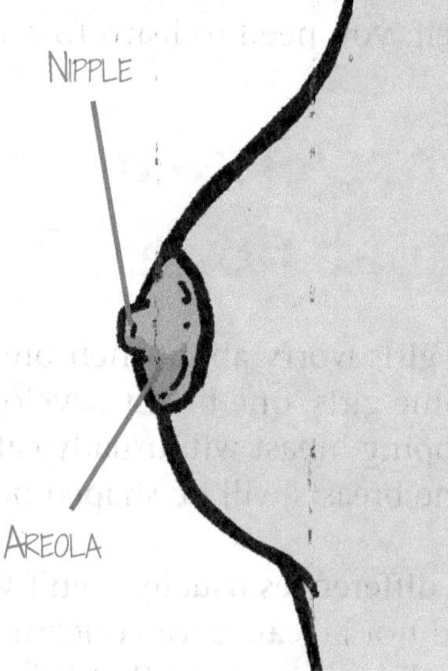

Nipples come in all sizes and colors. Some nipples are small, while others are large. Some nipples are light pink, others dark brown, and others a shade in between. The color of your nipples can depend on your skin color.

Some girls have inverted nipples. Inverted nipples turn inward instead of out. Although most girls who have inverted nipples have had them since birth, they may not become obvious until puberty. Sometimes inverted nipples turn out during puberty and then change back to inverted years later. Some women have inverted nipples throughout their lives. Inverted nipples are perfectly normal and nothing to be concerned about (although they can sometimes make breastfeeding a baby more difficult).

What if I have some hairs around my nipples?

You may notice hairs growing around your nipple area during puberty. These hairs are normal and common. It's best to leave them alone—pulling them out could irritate your skin.

How do I make sure my breasts are healthy?

As a teenager, you do not need to do anything to keep your breasts healthy. But when you get older—starting when you're about 18 years old—you will want to perform regular breast self-exams. Once a month, you will check your breasts for lumps or any changes. If you notice anything new, you should see your doctor to have it checked out and make sure it's nothing to worry about. Of course, you can start examining your breasts at any time now; the more familiar you are with your breasts, the more likely you'll be to discover anything new or unusual. It is very rare for lumps in girls your age to be anything to worry about. Also, as soon as you develop breasts, the doctor will start examining your breasts at each yearly exam.

But even at your age, you may notice things about your breasts that might concern you. Lumps often appear at certain times of the month—like right before your period, when your breasts may also be sore. This is caused by hormone changes during the menstrual cycle and is normal for many girls and women. But it's always safe to ask your doctor to check the lumps regularly to make sure they're not a problem.

Some girls notice a discharge, or fluid, coming from their nipples. If you notice a discharge from your nipples, it's a good idea to have it checked by the doctor, especially if the discharge is pink or contains pus (a thick, yellowish fluid that results from an infection).

When will I be ready to wear a bra?

When to start wearing a bra is a personal decision. You may feel ready and want to wear a bra when you first notice that your breasts are beginning to grow. Or you may want to wait until they're more developed. The bottom line: It's time to get your first bra whenever YOU are ready to.

How do I talk to my parents about bras?

If your parents don't talk to you about bras, don't hesitate to bring up the topic first. Your parents may not realize that you are ready to get a bra, or they may be waiting for you to ask for one. If you feel nervous, relax. Every girl has had or will have this conversation at some time in her life. Make it casual. Just let a trusted adult know that you feel ready to buy your first bra.

How do I know what size bra to get?

Bras come in a range of styles and sizes, represented by both a number and a letter. The number (usually between 28 and 40) has to do with the size of your rib cage and is the measurement of the band of the bra that goes from your chest around your back. To find out your number size, measure your rib cage (right below your breasts) with a tape measure from around your back to where the tape measure meets in the middle of your rib cage. Then add approximately 5 inches to this number.

The letter—usually between AA (the smallest) and D (the largest)—represents the size of the cups of the bra based on the size of your breasts. You can figure out your letter size by measuring your chest over your breasts at the nipples and around your back. Then subtract your rib cage measurement from this number. If the resulting number is 0, you are a size AA. If it is 1, you need an A cup. If it is 2, you need a B cup, and so on. Try on different bras to see how they fit or ask a salesperson in the bra section of a store to help you with this if you are having trouble. And don't be embarrassed. This is their job, and they're happy to do it.

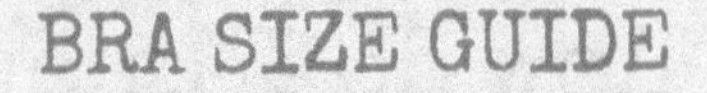

Measurement at rib cage in inches	Bra band size
22-23	28
24-25	30
26-27	32
28-29	34
30-31	36
32-33	38
34-35	40

Rib size	Breast Size	Cup Size
28	28	AA
28	29	A
28	30	B
28	31	C
28	32	D
28	33	DD

How do I know what kind of bra to get?

Stores sell many different types of bras, ranging from stretchy cotton training bras to sports bras to soft-cup, underwire, and push-up bras. Some attach in the front and some attach in the back; some are strapless. Try on a couple of different styles to see which fits you best and feels the most comfortable. You may want a sports bra for athletic activities and a different style bra for everyday wear. Don't hesitate to ask either the salesperson or a trusted adult for help.

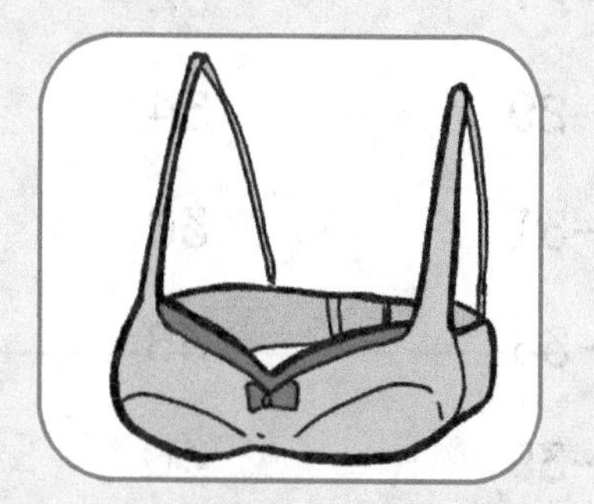

SOFT CUP BRAS: Soft cup bras have molded cups for the breasts. They help create a smooth, contoured appearance, but they do not have any lifting support. These comfortable bras are popular among smaller-chested girls and women or girls with more prominent nipples.

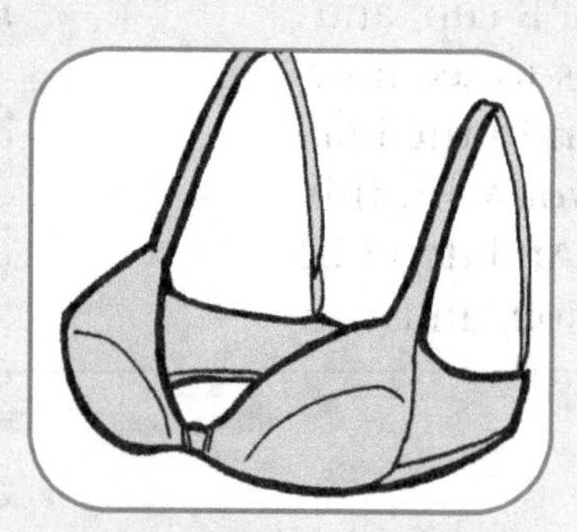

PADDED BRAS: Some girls and women wear padded bras to make their breasts appear larger. Padded bras have cups that are padded with fiberfill or other materials.

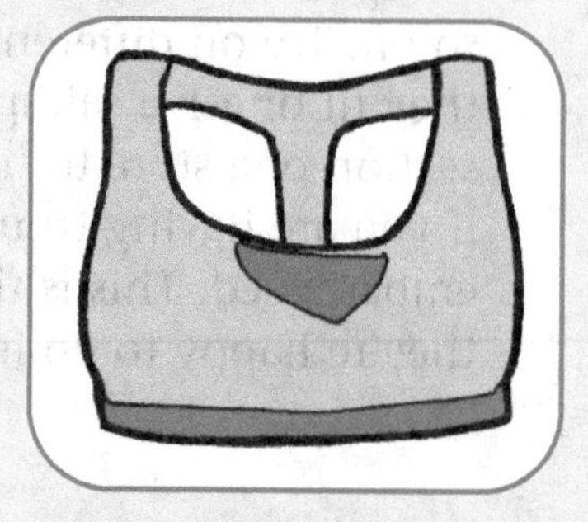

SPORTS BRAS: Perfect for active girls and women, sports bras have wide straps and cover a broader area of the chest. Sports bras hold breasts in place during exercise. Some sports bras are made of material that helps keep the skin dry.

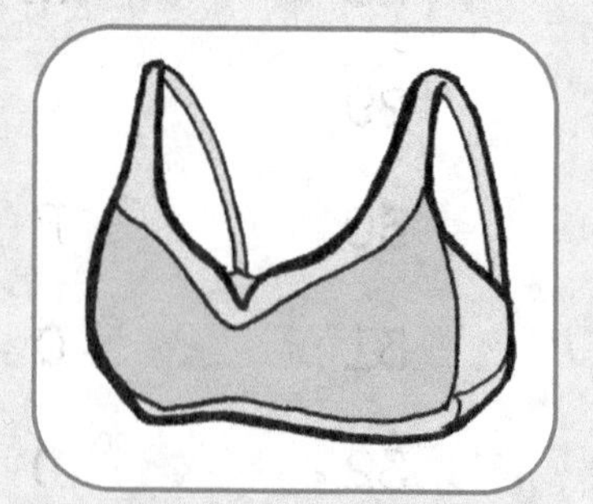

MINIMIZER BRAS: Girls and women with large breasts may prefer minimizer bras. Made of microfiber, minimizers hold the breasts close to the body to help make the bust line look smaller. They can also help make clothes fit better.

UNDERWIRE BRAS: This type of bra has a piece of wire beneath each breast that is made of flexible metal, plastic, or plastic-coated metal. Underwire bras provide support and help lift and separate the breasts. But unless they are the correct size, they can be uncomfortable.

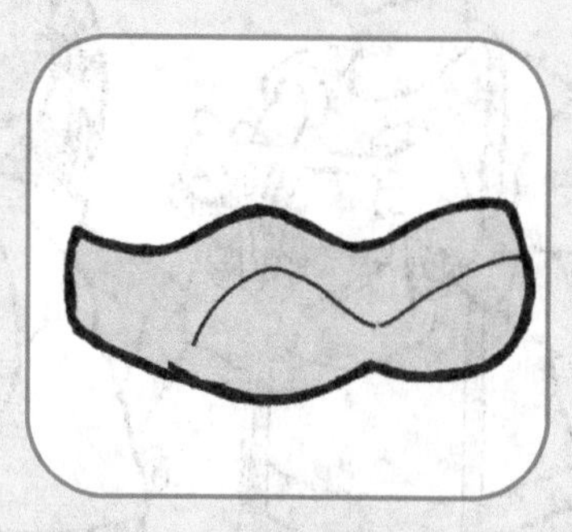

STRAPLESS BRAS: Although these bras don't have straps, they have wide sides and often have underwires beneath the breasts for support. Most strapless bras secure with triple hooks in the back. Many girls choose stretchy tube-style strapless bras because they are more comfortable.

What if I'm teased about my breasts?

Developing breasts can be an exciting part of puberty. It is great to feel positive about it! Unfortunately, some people may make comments about your breasts that embarrass or hurt you. This type of behavior is called sexual harassment and it is never okay. It makes girls feel self-conscious and it can even make some girls feel unsafe. You should not accept these kinds of comments. First, ask the person to stop. If that doesn't work, you can tell a trusted adult, like a parent. If it happens at school, tell someone who works there, such as a teacher, counselor, or the principal. If it's happening to you, it's probably happening to someone else.

The most important thing to know about your breasts is that their size has nothing to do with who you are as a person or how attractive you are. When you are feeling insecure about your breasts, remind yourself of all your wonderful qualities—both inside and out.

What are the reproductive organs?

Most of your reproductive *organs* are inside your body. Even those parts outside can be hard to see. The parts outside are called the *genitals*. You might want to take a look at them by using a small mirror placed between your legs. This is easy to do when you're sitting with your knees bent out to the sides and your feet crossed. Try not to feel uncomfortable or embarrassed doing this. After all, it's your body, and it is natural to be curious. It's good to know as much as you can about your body.

What am I looking at?

When you're looking at your genital area, you are seeing the *vulva*, which is the name for the entire outer, visible genital area. The vulva is made up of different parts. At the top of the vulva is the *mons*, a small, rounded pad of fat that lies over the pubic bone.

Below the mons are the *labia*, or lips. You have two sets of lips, inner (*labia minora*) and outer (*labia majora*). The outer lips are where your first pubic hairs will grow. Outer and inner labia are different in size, shape, and color in each person. One more thing that makes each person unique! The inner and outer lips grow and change during puberty.

At the top of the inner labia is the *clitoris*, a small, pea-sized bump. The clitoris can be covered by the top of your inner lips, which is called the hood. The clitoris is a very sexually sensitive organ, and touching it can feel good or even uncomfortable. Your clitoris will grow a bit bigger as you get older.

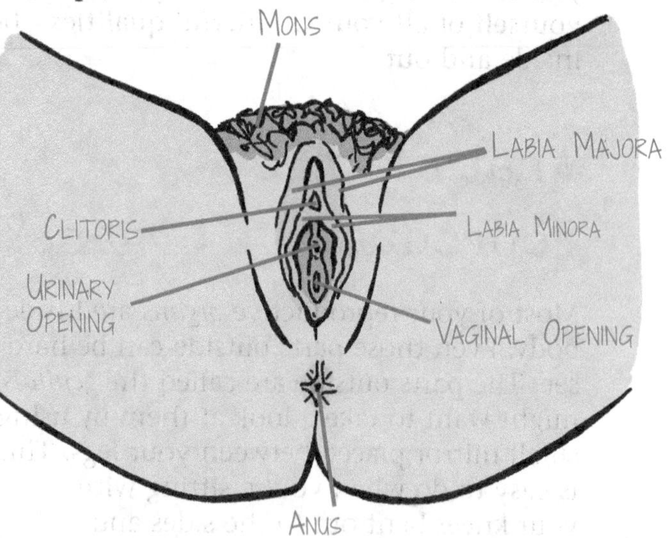

Just below the clitoris is the *urinary opening*, through which urine leaves the body. The *vaginal opening* is below the urinary opening and is larger than the urinary opening. Your vaginal opening will get larger during puberty. At the vaginal opening is a thin layer of tissue called the *hymen*. Contrary to popular belief, the hymen does not cover the entire vaginal opening. The hymen may stretch or tear from vigorous exercise or sexual intercourse.

Behind the vaginal opening toward your buttocks you'll see another opening. This is the *anus*, which, like the urinary opening, is not part of the reproductive system. It is from the anus that solid waste leaves your body.

What are my internal reproductive organs?

The rest of your reproductive organs are on the inside of your body. You are born with all of these organs but it is not until puberty that these organs become mature and capable of reproducing. But this certainly doesn't mean you're ready to be a parent!

If you could see inside your body, this is what you would see:

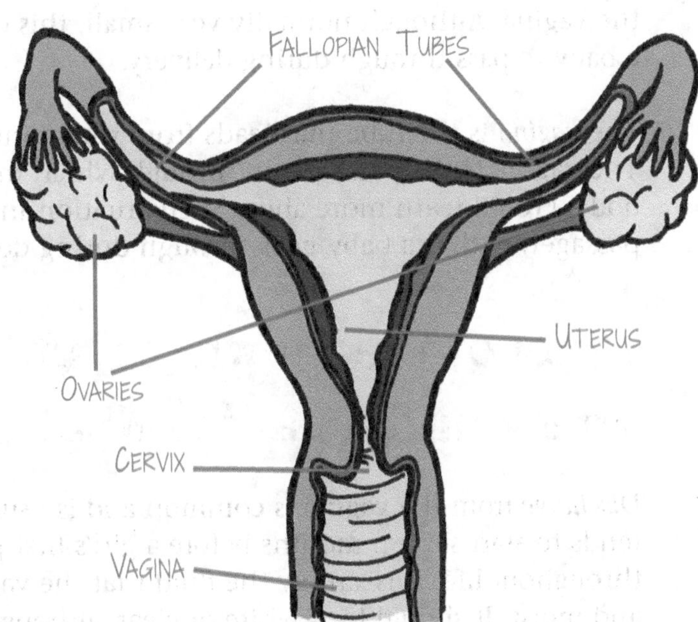

You have two *ovaries*, one on each side of your body. Inside the ovaries are eggs, which are called ova. Your ovaries contain hundreds of thousands of eggs, with which you were born.

Two tubes, called *fallopian tubes*, stretch from your ovaries to the uterus (which you will learn about in the next paragraph). The fallopian tubes are about 3 to 4 inches long. When an egg is released from one of your ovaries, it travels inside a fallopian tube to the uterus.

> The ovaries produce estrogen, the major female sex hormone. Estrogen is the hormone that is making your body start to look more like that of a woman. The ovaries also produce a small amount of the male sex hormone testosterone.

In the center of your *pelvis* is the *uterus*, which grows to the size and shape of a small pear. The uterus has thick, muscular walls and is empty on the inside. It joins with the fallopian tubes at the top on each side and the cervix at the bottom (see the next paragraph). During pregnancy, a fetus grows and develops inside the uterus. (The uterus stretches and grows to accommodate the growing fetus.)

The *cervix* is the bottom part of the uterus. The cervix has a small opening into the vagina. Although normally very small, this opening can stretch enough for a baby to pass through during delivery.

The *vagina* is the tube that leads from the uterus to the outside of the body. The vagina is the passageway through which menstrual blood leaves the body. (You'll learn more about menstruation in the next chapter.) It's also the passageway that a baby goes through during delivery.

I've noticed a white, sticky substance in my underpants. What is it?

Discharge from the vagina is common and is usually nothing to worry about. It tends to start several months before a girl's first period and continues throughout life. It is simply the fluid that the vagina makes to keep itself clean and moist. It should look white or clear, although when it dries on your underpants it may look a little yellow.

Vaginal discharge can change in amount and consistency over the course of the month because of the menstrual cycle. There will be less of it at times and more at others. This is also normal. You only need to worry about discharge if your vagina becomes itchy or irritated, if the discharge has a strong odor, or if the color changes from white or clear to dark yellow or greenish. If you notice any of these changes, you may have an infection and you will need to go to the doctor to have it checked out. (As part of your yearly routine physical examinations, the doctor will examine your external genitals to make sure everything is healthy.)

I've noticed that when I touch myself down there it feels good. Is this okay?

Touching your body in this way is called *masturbation*. You are touching the clitoris, which is very sensitive tissue that is involved with sexual arousal. You cannot hurt yourself by masturbating. Most people masturbate at some time in their life, and this is a perfectly healthy, normal activity that helps you learn more about your body and its responses. It's also okay to choose not to masturbate if you don't want to.

I worry that my vaginal area smells bad. Should I use one of the feminine hygiene sprays or douches that I see in the drugstore?

You do not need to use any kind of vaginal deodorant products or douches because your vagina cleanses itself. Deodorant sprays can cause irritation, redness, or swelling in the genital area; douches can contribute to vaginal infections by reducing the helpful bacteria that are normally present in your vagina to keep it healthy.

To prevent genital odors, shower or take a bath every day and wear underwear that is clean and not too tight. Cotton underwear (or at least with cotton in the crotch) is best because cotton allows air to circulate and helps keep the area drier.

If you notice an unusual, unpleasant, or very strong odor in your vaginal area, you may have an infection. In this case, you need to see your doctor.

Chapter Six:

Your Period

In the previous chapter you read about your ovaries and the eggs they contain. Approximately once a month one of your ovaries releases an egg. The egg travels from the ovary into the connecting fallopian tube and through the fallopian tube into your uterus. (In order for you to become pregnant, the egg would need to be fertilized by a *sperm* cell inside the fallopian tube.)

Every month your uterus gets ready for a possible pregnancy. The lining in the wall of the uterus gets thicker so that a fertilized egg will have a place to grow and develop. The lining, which is called the *endometrium,* is made up of blood and tissue. If the egg is not fertilized, the uterus does not need all the extra lining—so the lining dissolves and leaves the body through the vagina in the form of blood. This is called *menstruation,* or more commonly, a *period*.

What is the menstrual cycle?

Your *menstrual cycle* is the activity going on inside your body before, during, and in between periods. The length of your cycle is the number of days from the first day of one period to the first day of the next period.

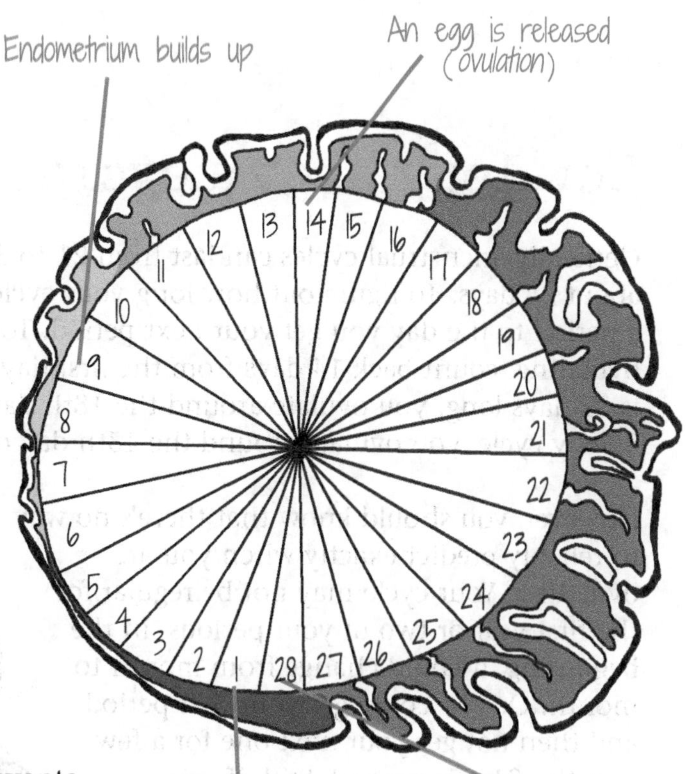

This chart shows you the approximate times when these events occur during the menstrual cycle.

- On day 1, you get your period.
- About 5 to 7 days after your period starts, the lining of the uterus (the endometrium) begins to build up.
- About midway through your cycle, usually around day 14 (or, more precisely, 14 days before your next period), one of your ovaries releases an egg into a fallopian tube. This release of an egg from an ovary is called *ovulation* . It is while the egg travels through the fallopian tube, which takes about 5 to 7 days, that the egg is most likely to be fertilized.
- If the egg has not been fertilized within 5 to 7 days after ovulation, it breaks up in the fallopian tube or uterus.
- At about day 28 of your cycle, the thickened endometrium breaks down and prepares to leave your body in the form of menstrual blood. This is the start of another period and another menstrual cycle.

How long does a cycle last?

Generally, menstrual cycles can last from 21 to 35 days. The average cycle is about 28 days. To figure out how long your cycle is, count from the first day of a period to the day you get your next period. To figure out when you are ovulating, count back 14 days from the first day of your period. So, if your cycle is 32 days long, you ovulate around the 18th day of your cycle. If you have a 27-day cycle, you ovulate around the 13th day of your cycle.

However, you should know that there's no way to reliably predict exactly when you are ovulating. Your cycle may not be regular for the first year or two of your periods. In the beginning, it could change from month to month. Or you could get your first period and then not get your next one for a few months. This is normal. Still, if you have any questions or if you still have irregular periods more than two years after you start having periods, talk to a trusted adult or your doctor.

Psssst! To learn more about your menstrual cycle, keep track of your periods on a calendar.

Pssst! Getting your first period is a major sign that you are growing up physically!

How might I feel about getting my period?

You might feel several ways at once about getting your period—excited, nervous, curious about what to expect, or even a little annoyed that you have to be bothered by the whole thing. But getting your period is another healthy, natural development that occurs during puberty. Regular periods are a sign of hormone balance inside your body, which is also very important for keeping your bones strong.

When will I get my first period?

There is no way to predict exactly when you will get your first period. Most girls get it sometime between ages 9 and 15. Girls usually get their period about 2 years after they start to develop breasts. Ask your mom and older sisters when they got their first period, because heredity is a factor in when you will get yours. If you're worried about not having your period yet, or if you don't have it by the time you're 16, talk to your doctor.

A girl's period can be irregular during the first few years. You may miss your period for 1 or even 2 months, or at other times you may have two periods close together.

How long will my period last?

Your period will usually last somewhere between 2 and 8 days. For most girls, it lasts about 5 days.

How much blood should I expect?

At times it can feel like there is a lot of blood leaving your body during your period. In reality, it is only a few tablespoons—usually no more than 1 or 2 ounces of fluid during a whole period.

Should I use pads or tampons?

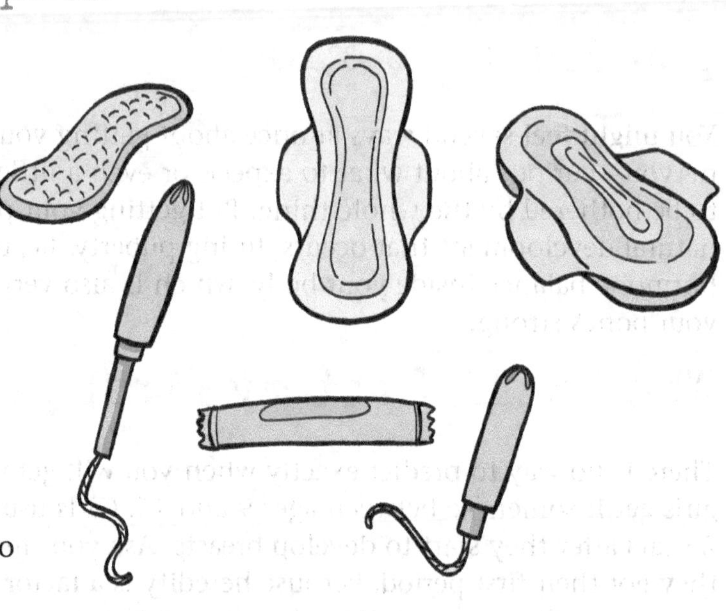

Whether to use pads or tampons is a personal choice. Both work equally well. *Sanitary pads* are made of material that is good at absorbing fluid. Pads have an adhesive strip on the bottom and some also have adhesive strips on the sides that stick to your underpants to keep the pad in place.

Tampons are made of cotton that is rolled into a tube. They usually come in a cardboard or plastic applicator that you use to insert the tampon into your vagina. If you feel uncomfortable about inserting a tampon into your vagina, you may want to use pads. But if you play a lot of sports, like to go swimming, or feel that pads are too "messy," you may want to use tampons, which stay inside your body. Many girls and women use both pads and tampons, depending on the situation.

MYTHBUSTER

You cannot "break your hymen" (tear the tissue) or lose your virginity by using tampons. Tampons do not change your body in any way—your vaginal opening can stretch easily for a tampon. Although you can tear your hymen through vigorous exercise, the only way you can lose your virginity is to have sexual intercourse for the first time.

Tampons and pads come in all different sizes and types. It can be pretty confusing the first time you go into a store and see the shelves filled with so many options. This is another time when it helps to talk to a trusted adult or older girl about all of these choices. They can help you figure out which option will work best for you.

What do I do when I get my period for the first time?

It's a good idea to be prepared for your first period ahead of time. You may want to keep some pads in your locker at school or in your backpack in case you're not at home when you get your first period. Talk to a trusted adult about your feelings and concerns. Getting your period can feel like a very big deal and it helps to be able to talk openly about it. The person you talk to will probably be able to help you get some of the supplies you'll need, such as pads or tampons.

If you're at school when you get your first period and you don't have the supplies you need, the school nurse will be able to help you. If you get your period outside of school and you aren't able to ask anyone for a pad, simply put a wad of toilet paper in your underwear until you get home.

How often do I need to change my tampon or pad?

You should use a new pad whenever you need to, depending on how heavy your blood flow is. Even if you don't need to change your pad, you may want to change it every 6 to 8 hours for hygiene reasons.

It's especially important to change tampons regularly even when your period is not heavy because keeping one in too long could cause a rare but serious infection called *toxic shock syndrome*. As long as you change your tampons frequently—at least every 4 to 8 hours—you don't need to worry about infection. It's also a good idea to use tampons with the lowest absorbency you need. Some girls prefer to use pads overnight.

Make sure you carry some pads or tampons with you during your entire period!

I keep hearing about PMS. What is it?

PMS stands for *premenstrual syndrome*. Your hormones fluctuate throughout the menstrual cycle. These hormone changes can affect the way you feel, both physically and emotionally.

If you have any questions or concerns about your period, ask your mother or another trusted adult, an older sister or girlfriend, the school nurse, or your doctor. There is no such thing as a "stupid" question. The more you know, the more in control you are and the less you will worry.

You might feel extra tired or you might have *cramps* in your pelvic area or lower back before, during, or right after your period. Your skin might break out during the week or so before your period. You may notice that your mood seems to shift and you feel unusually crabby, mopey, or sad.

All of these symptoms are normal, but it's important not to let them ruin your day (or your week!). It always helps to talk to someone close to you about how you are feeling.

I have really bad cramps when I get my period. What can I do?

Some girls find that aerobic exercise such as jogging helps relieve their cramps. Other girls find that taking a warm bath or placing a heating pad on their pelvic area helps. Ask your doctor about using an over-the-counter pain medication. It's not uncommon for girls to have diarrhea or feel sick to their stomach during their period. If the pain or cramps are so bad that you miss school or other activities, or if your periods are extremely heavy and you get more tired than usual, see your doctor.

Pssst! Try limiting the amount of sugar you eat and being more active in the days leading up to your period. Diet and exercise play a major role in how you feel!

Chapter Seven:
Your Feelings

When you were younger, you experienced all kinds of feelings—you were happy a lot of the time, sometimes you were scared or angry, and occasionally you felt stressed or overwhelmed.

The difference when you get to be a teenager is that these feelings can seem to switch from one minute to the next. Sometimes they even seem to happen all at once. And sometimes you experience a really strong feeling, like anger, without even knowing why.

This can be confusing. But it's important to know that these changes in mood and emotions are a normal part of being a teenager.

What is causing these changes in my mood?

Your hormones are a major cause of all these mood changes you are experiencing. Your hormones are changing a lot during this time in your life. Just as hormones affect many activities in your body, they can affect the way you feel. You are probably also going through some big changes in your life. You may have started middle school. You may have made new friends or ended some old friendships as your interests have changed. You may have started to develop a crush on, or romantic feelings toward, someone. You may notice that you feel ready to take on some new responsibilities, privileges, and freedoms. Your parents may not always agree with you. All of these life changes can affect your mood.

Will I have trouble controlling my moods?

Your mood may change frequently during puberty. One minute you might be giggling with girlfriends over something silly and the next minute you might be crying. This shift in emotions can be pretty exhausting. Learning about different feelings and ways to handle them can make life easier. Remember that you really are ready to handle these new grown-up ways of feeling and thinking and that they will become easier to deal with as you get older.

What can I do when I'm not feeling very good about myself?

You are going through so many changes at once, and you may notice that you sometimes don't feel as good about yourself as you did when you were younger. This can be the result of comparing yourself to others. Or you may be spending more time worrying about how you look or what other people think about you.

Sometimes you might hear a little voice in your head saying things like "You can't do that—no one thinks you're smart enough, talented enough, pretty enough." This is called negative self-talk. Negative self-talk happens when you tell yourself discouraging things that make you feel bad. Doing this can take away your self-confidence and make you stop trying new things. It could even make you turn away from friends and stay more to yourself.

Put a stop to any negative self-talking! Every time you find yourself saying something negative, turn it around into something positive. For example, instead of thinking "I'm not going to try out for the school soccer team because I'm not fast enough," try thinking something positive instead like "I'm going to try. If I work hard, there's no reason I can't improve my running speed and make the team!"

It's important to practice changing negative statements into positive ones. The more you do this, the easier it will get. If you have been trying this strategy for a while and still find yourself overwhelmed by negative self-talk, it's time to talk to a trusted adult such as a parent or another older relative, a favorite counselor or teacher, or your doctor.

All of a sudden my relationship with my parents has changed. What's happening?

Every girl's relationship with her parents changes during puberty. You may want more independence and you may feel ready to make more decisions for yourself—like what clothes to wear, what to eat, when to do your homework, when to go to bed at night, and how much time to spend with your friends. Your parents might not always agree that you are ready to make these decisions on your own. Keep in mind that your parents are going through their own changes as you grow!

It's normal for teenagers to have more disagreements with their parents than they did when they were younger. Just because your relationship with your parents is changing doesn't mean it has to change in a negative way.

Communication is so essential at this time in your life that it is well worth working on. You and your parents will feel better and can deepen your relationship if you do a lot of both talking and listening to each other. Try to appreciate that your parents care deeply about you and are doing their best to help you become a happy, responsible adult.

How can I communicate better with my parents?

Here are some tips for improving your communication with your parents:

* ***Plan ahead*** Find a time and a place when you can really spend some time sorting through an issue you're concerned about—for example, when you and a parent are out for lunch or dinner, relaxing at home, or on a long car ride. (Sitting in the car outside school as the bell is ringing is not a good time for an important discussion.)

* ***Prioritize*** Figure out which issues are most important. If what you are hoping to achieve is some extra time with your friends after school, don't bring up other requests at the same time. Save those for another time.

* ***Negotiate*** See if after you do something your parents have asked you to do then you are allowed to do something you would like to do. If you're working on getting more privileges and freedom, you can increase your chances by showing your parents that you are more responsible. For example, take more responsibility for getting all of your homework done without having to be reminded, or for chores like cleaning your room and doing your laundry. When your parents see you acting more grown-up and independent, they may be more likely to agree that you are ready for more privileges.

* ***Compromise*** For example, if you want freedom to spend more time with your friends and your parents are willing to allow you more time on the weekends but not on school nights, this might be a good compromise.

* ***Take turns*** Agree to take turns listening and talking. Neither of you can get your point across when you're talking at the same time. Practice the 5-second rule with your parents: You each wait 5 seconds before responding to the other.

How do I handle feeling angry?

Another feeling that you are probably experiencing is anger. It is normal to feel angry sometimes. Perhaps somebody hurt your feelings or you didn't get to do something that you really wanted to do. So, you get angry. Maybe you yell, storm out of a room, or slam a door. Or maybe you react in the opposite way—you don't express your angry feelings and you hold them inside.

Adolescence is a good time to learn new ways of coping with angry feelings. If you hold your angry feelings inside, you may find that they seep out in other ways. You might get headaches or stomachaches, or you may start to feel really down or tired all the time. You might even turn your anger against yourself and do something self-destructive. It's essential and healthy to let angry feelings out.

On the other hand, you want to try not to let your anger out in an aggressive way. By yelling or slamming doors, you can hurt someone and make the situation worse.

If you find that you're having a hard time getting your angry feelings to go away, it may be time to talk to someone who can help you. A school counselor, your doctor, or another trusted adult would be happy to help you figure out some other ways to cope with your angry feelings.

Here are some tips for handling angry feelings:

* Talk about your feelings using "I" statements. Start with "I feel angry because...." Don't accuse the other person of having done something. Instead, focus on your own feelings.

* Talk about what would help make you feel better. Try something like "I would feel less angry if we didn't call each other hurtful names."

* Avoid talking directly with the person who made you feel angry until you've cooled off.

Here are some tips to help you calm down:

* Do something physical. Go for a long walk, jog, or a bike ride.

* Write down how you feel. A journal is a great place to express yourself.

* Do something relaxing. Listen to your favorite CD, take a bath, or watch some television.

* Let your feelings out. Scream into a pillow, cry, or call a friend.

What can I do about my shyness?

Some girls find that being shy is especially difficult during the teen years. It can feel harder to make new friends or to participate in school activities like dances or parties.

If you tend to be shy, here are some ways of coping:

Don't get frustrated. Many people find it hard to be outgoing. It's a skill that you can learn, like all of the other things you've learned to do over the years. Start small. Decide to say hello to a couple of different people in the hall at school, or invite a new friend over to your house.

Find ways to get involved in conversations and activities. Ask a friend to introduce you to someone new. Or join a club or a team so you will have something in common to talk about with a group of people.

It may feel scary at first to be more outgoing, but it will get easier. And remember that no one knows how you feel inside. You may be feeling terribly nervous, but if you keep a smile on your face and a friendly tone in your voice, others will see you only as nice, not shy.

Does this ever happen to you?

You feel like you've said the wrong thing to someone and can't stop worrying about it. Unless you've been mean and hurt someone's feelings (in which case you can apologize to the person), keep in mind that other people won't remember what you said the way you do—or for nearly as long. You can just let it go.

REAL GiRLS, REAL FEELiNGS

"There's a girl that I thought was my friend, but when I would try to talk to her she always ignored me when other people were around. It made me feel bad, but then I realized that she was not a true friend, so I looked for other kids who like to do the same things I do." Age 10

"Sometimes I go to the school social worker when I'm angry. She helps me deal with my feelings in a good way and things don't seem so bad anymore." Age 13

"I have always been tough, strong, and able to take almost anything. But now it seems I'm more sensitive and my feelings get hurt more easily. My mom says it's because of all the changes my body is going through and that underneath all the emotional stuff I'm still the same strong person I always was." Age 12

"I didn't used to talk much about my feelings and kept things to myself because I was afraid that if I opened up people would think I was strange or wouldn't like me. But little by little, I'm talking more about my feelings and finding out that it helps. Now I know that other people have the same feelings I do." Age 10

"I get mad really easily and it really upsets me because I didn't used to get mad so much." Age 11

"I'm liking middle school because it's not just the kids from my neighborhood anymore. A lot of the new kids in middle school are different from my other friends but they're still a lot like me." Age 11

I'm feeling so stressed out! What can I do?

It's easy to feel more stress as you become a teen. You may have more homework, more after-school activities, more responsibilities at home, and more conflicts with your friends or parents. All of these things can make you feel a little overwhelmed at times.

When you find yourself feeling overloaded with work or stressed out, it's time to figure out some ways to relax. Here are some simple tips to help you feel less stressed:

- Do an activity that makes you feel good. This can be anything from drawing or reading to exercising, playing a sport or game with some friends, or playing with the dog. No matter how busy you are, you need to always make time for some fun stuff just for you!

- Do something calming. Play soft music, listen to a meditation tape, or follow a yoga video.

- Take extra good care of your body. Eat nutritious foods, get plenty of sleep, and avoid things like caffeine that can make you feel nervous.

- Talk to people. They might help you see your stresses in a new light. Maybe a friend has felt the same way and has some good advice. You just may find that what you're worrying about isn't such a big problem after all.

I've been feeling down lately. Should I be worried?

When you're feeling sad, try to cheer yourself up with positive thoughts. It always helps to look at the bright side of things!

Everyone experiences sadness at times. If you get a bad grade, have an argument with a friend, or don't make a team you tried out for, chances are you will feel sad. Feelings of sadness usually go away pretty quickly. You may feel down for a day or two, and then you suddenly start to feel better.

For some people, though, it's harder to get rid of sad feelings. If you have some of the following symptoms for 2 weeks or longer, you may be experiencing depression:

- You feel sad most of the time.
- You aren't as interested in your hobbies as you used to be.
- You feel bad about yourself most of the time.
- You feel tired most of the time.
- Your sleep and eating patterns have changed.
- You feel that it's harder than usual to concentrate.
- You often feel irritable, sometimes even with friends.
- You can't imagine you will ever feel better.

If you are experiencing a few of these symptoms, tell a trusted adult immediately. He or she will help you figure out what you can do to feel better.

If you ever feel like hurting yourself or feel that life is not worth living, you need to get help right away. Tell your parents or another trusted adult immediately. No one should have to feel that down, and there are things that can be done to help you start feeling better.

My grandmother recently died and I'm confused about what I'm feeling.

You are probably feeling grief. Grief is a strong feeling of sadness that people experience when someone close to them dies. You can also experience grief at other times, such as when you lose your best friend or a pet dies. You may be feeling sad, hopeless, lonely, scared, confused, or guilty—or all of those at different times. It helps to talk about your feelings with other family members who are also experiencing the loss. It can also help to talk with other people who have lost a loved one. You will realize that you are not alone—other people have similar feelings.

Everyone experiences grief in his or her own way but most people tend to follow a common pattern. At first, many people have a feeling of numbness because they are having a hard time accepting the death and they may even deny it for awhile. They may feel alone, empty, and in shock during this first stage of grief. Then, they may begin to feel guilty and angry, and they may even take their anger out on the people who are closest to them. In the next stage, people usually experience intense feelings of sadness and loneliness. After a time, these intense feelings begin to calm down and they start to gradually return to their normal routine.

The final stage of grief is when you are able to accept the death and begin to enjoy your friends and activities again. You will still think about your grandmother, but with less pain. Eventually, you will be able to remember her with happiness.

My parents recently told me that they're separating. What can I do?

It's very challenging for teenagers when parents separate, divorce, begin dating someone new, have more children with a new partner, or bring stepchildren into the family. In these circumstances, it's normal for teenagers to experience extreme emotions. If you're going through changes like these at home, you may feel angry, scared, lonely, or confused, or even guilty.

Remember that many kids go through these changes, and it can help to talk to other kids who are experiencing the same things as you. It's also essential to talk to your parents about how you are coping with all of these changes. You don't always have to put on a brave face—your parents don't expect you to be strong all the time. They know that sometimes you may need to cry, yell, or just talk it out.

If you are finding that your feelings are becoming overwhelming, your grades are slipping, you feel irritable most of the time, or you are having trouble sleeping, you need to confide in a trusted adult. He or she can help you figure out some ways to cope during this difficult period.

Why should I tell other people about my feelings?

You can expect to have all kinds of feelings over the next few years—and for the rest of your life. You will have some of your happiest and proudest moments as you achieve new accomplishments and experience new pleasures. You may also have some low moments. Ideally, the low times will pass quickly. But remember that we all need to talk to other people about our feelings. Reaching out for support from other people is actually a sign of strength—not weakness.

You should know that the adults you trust—such as your parents, your doctor, or your school counselor or teacher—will keep whatever you tell them confidential if you ask them to, as long as the information does not affect your or a friend's safety. From now on at your regular doctor visits, your doctor is likely to ask your parent to leave the room so you and the doctor can talk alone. The doctor will want to ask you if there is anything you want to talk about, such as things that are bothering you or questions you want to ask. He or she will also ask you about ways you may be keeping yourself healthy or putting yourself at risk. Keep in mind that the doctor talks to many young people your age and has heard all kinds of things and answered all kinds of questions. The doctor will not share what you say with your parents or anyone else, unless you tell him or her something that indicates you are in danger.

Chapter Eight:

Relationships

You will probably notice that your relationships will change a lot during your teenage years. Who your friends are and how much time you spend with them might feel more important to you than before. You may also find that you don't want your parents to be as involved in your day-to-day life as they used to be. These changes are normal. Still, they are certainly worth examining more closely.

Pssst! Remember that developing a friendship takes time—but a brief conversation is a great start!

What makes a good friend?

Good friends come in all kinds of packages. Still, most good friends have one or more important qualities such as those described below.

A good friend...

...is someone you can count on.

...is considerate of your feelings.

...listens when you need to talk.

...makes you feel good about yourself.

...likes some or many of the same things you do.

...may have some differences from you, but it doesn't affect your relationship.

...considers what is best for you.

How can I find a good friend?

Keep your eyes and your mind open, because you never know where or when you'll find a good friend. It could be just about anywhere and any time! One easy way is to find someone who shares your interests. If you like to play sports, join a team. If you're interested in art, join an art group or take art classes in your community.

If you see someone you'd like to meet, approach the person and say a friendly "hello." Then maybe ask a question that will help you get to know him or her better, like "What do you think of that new teacher?" or "Have you seen that new movie yet?" or "Have you done that math assignment yet?"

How can I keep a good friend?

Look back at the good friend list on page 87. Now ask yourself, do you have those qualities yourself? In order to have and keep good friends, you also need to be a good friend. You need to be there for your friends—ready to listen and support them. You need to be trustworthy and honest. Last but not least, accept your friends for who they are and work hard to sort through disagreements you may have with them.

What should I do if I have a fight with a friend?

Disagreeing with friends every once in while is normal. No matter how close you are, you are not always going to see things exactly the same way.

When you have a disagreement with a friend, talk about it. Sometimes friends don't feel comfortable telling each other when they're angry or upset about something. The angry feelings start to build and before you know it these feelings cause a big fight. Or, if you wait too long to talk, you and your friend may end up giving up on the friendship entirely.

Problems usually start out small—sometimes a fight begins with a simple misunderstanding. If you talk about it, you might find that you can resolve the issue quickly. Listening is very important when talking through a disagreement. Be sure to listen carefully to each other—that's the best way to work out a solution.

What should I do if I notice that a friend is growing apart from me?

Growing apart happens in some friendships. As you get older, you may discover that you have less in common with a friend than you did when you were younger. Maybe all of a sudden one of you is making new friends and isn't interested in spending as much time together anymore. It can be very upsetting to have this happen to you. You may feel left out and alone.

Try to talk to your friend and let her know how you're feeling. She may not realize the effect her actions are having on you. Or you may be right that she is trying to get some distance in your relationship. If this is the case, you may need to just let it be.

This is a good time to focus on developing other friendships. Talk to your parents or another trusted adult or another friend about how you are feeling. It's okay to be sad and angry when a friendship ends, but remember that you will feel better over time!

What should I do if I have a friend who acts a lot older or younger than I do?

As you read earlier in the book, every girl goes through puberty in her own unique way. You may be a girl who is ready to act like a teenager. You may be interested in reading different kinds of books than you read when you were younger, seeing different kinds of movies, going to parties, and wearing the latest fashion. Or you may still feel more like a kid than a teenager. You may still enjoy playing with games and toys you've liked for the past couple of years.

It's hard when a friendship ends, but it's also a normal part of growing up.

It can be a challenge for a friendship to survive when one friend is following new interests and the other is still having fun with old activities. Sometimes these friendships do work because underneath it all the two friends still have enough in common that they enjoy each other's company. Often, friends can respect and accept the differences between them. Other times, these friendships just don't seem to work so well anymore. In this situation, it may be better for both friends to work on developing different friendship groups, ones in which they will feel more understood and accepted.

What is bullying?

When people think of *bullying,* they often picture a bigger kid forcing a smaller kid to give up his or her lunch money. That is an example of bullying, but there are a lot of other ways that people are bullied. Teasing, threatening, or purposely leaving another person out are also forms of bullying, as are telling stories and gossiping about someone.

Bullies aren't necessarily strangers or kids who are not your friends. Many girls report being bullied by their friends. For example, let's say that your friend invites a group of girls over to her house for a sleepover and purposely doesn't include you; this may be an act of bullying. Maybe a friend tells your secret to a group of kids you didn't want to know about it. That's bullying, too.

Many girls report that they are bullied in school—where, for example, rumors are spread about them, they are told they can no longer sit at their usual cafeteria table, or they stop receiving invitations to parties.

Other girls say that they have been bullied on the Internet. They say that other girls have sent e-mails or instant messages spreading rumors or false information about them.

What should I do if I am or a friend is being bullied?

Bullying is *never* acceptable. And bullying is very hard to deal with alone. If you are the victim of bullying, tell your parents, a teacher or school counselor, or some friends. You need all the help and support you can get when responding to a bully.

Some kids try to ignore bullies. After all, bullies are trying to get your attention. If you don't give them the attention they want, they may become bored and stop picking on you. But if this doesn't work, you need to get other people involved to help you.

It's easy to feel embarrassed when you're being bullied. But you're not the one who should feel embarrassed. The bully should be embarrassed and ashamed. No one deserves to be bullied—no matter what!

If you have a friend who is being bullied, it's important to stand up for her or him. Let the person being bullied know that you are there to help. If you see someone being bullied, try intervening by just walking over and helping the victim walk away.

If one of your friends is being the bully, try to talk to him or her. Let him or her know that you don't like what he or she is doing. This isn't always easy to do because you risk losing your friendship, but it's courageous. It's also the right thing to do—for both the person being bullied and your friend.

Could I be a bully?

Are you critical of others or do you look for faults in other people? Do you make fun of people? Have you purposely left out other kids or spread rumors about other kids? If so, you have acted like a bully.

It can be hard to stop doing these things, but you will feel better about yourself if you do. Sometimes girls bully other girls because they think it will make them more popular. You may have more friends who are scared to stand up to you, but do they really like you if you are treating them badly? It is much better to have friends who stick by you because they truly like you and feel supported by you. And in the long run, they will be better friends to you too.

If you are having a hard time stopping yourself from being a bully, you need to talk to someone. Start with your parents or a school counselor. They can help you figure out some ways to form healthier relationships.

I keep hearing about peer pressure. What is it?

People who are your age, like your classmates, are called your peers. Because you spend so much time with your peers, you naturally learn from each other. When you influence each other to do something, it's called *peer pressure*. Peer pressure can be either positive or negative.

Positive peer pressure is when someone influences you in a positive, constructive way, like studying hard, being kind to older people, helping out at home, and avoiding alcohol and drugs. Positive peer pressure is a very good thing.

Negative peer pressure is when someone tries to get you to do something you know you shouldn't do, like cheating on a test, drinking alcohol, cutting class, lying to your parents, or shoplifting. This pressure may come in the form of bribes, dares, nagging, or even threats.

It may not seem possible at your age, but the choices you make at this time in your life can have a lasting impact—both good and bad—on your future. So think hard before you act—and try to make good choices!

Even if other kids are not obviously trying to get you to do something, you may give in to peer pressure on your own and smoke cigarettes or do something else unhealthy because you want to be accepted by the group or "fit in." Or maybe you're afraid that the kids in the group will make fun of you if you don't go along. It's important to learn how to resist giving in to peer pressure that can be harmful. The next couple of questions will give you some ideas on how to make good choices.

Some of my friends have started shoplifting. They keep asking me to do it with them but I don't want to. What should I do?

Deep down, you know that stealing is wrong and you don't want to get in trouble. You also don't want your parents to be disappointed in you. But keep in mind that the consequences of shoplifting can have a lasting effect on you—it's simply not worth it to allow yourself to be pressured into doing something you know is wrong.

Tell your friends there's no way you're going to risk getting into trouble. You can also suggest something else to do, or say you need to get home and you're already late. Or simply walk away from the situation.

In the end, if your friends really care about you, they will respect that you need to make your own decisions. Also, good friends don't want their friends to get into trouble and should support them when they decide they don't want to do something they know is wrong. This group of kids may not be the best choice in friends. You may want to find friends who share your values and don't try to get you to do things you know are wrong.

REAL GiRLS, REAL FEELiNGS

"A friend told me her boyfriend kept trying to get her to do sexual stuff with him. She said he stopped after she told him that if he really liked her, he wouldn't force her to do things she's not ready to do. Now they get along better." Age 13

"There's a boy in my class who always tries to talk to me. I think he likes me but I don't like him that way. I don't know how to tell him without hurting his feelings." Age 12

"Some of the kids that I hang out with are starting to drink or smoke. I have started hanging out with a different group of friends because I'm not into that." Age 12

"One of my best friends is a bully and it makes me really nervous to be around her when she's picking on someone. I want her to like me, but I think I'm going to say something about it." Age 11

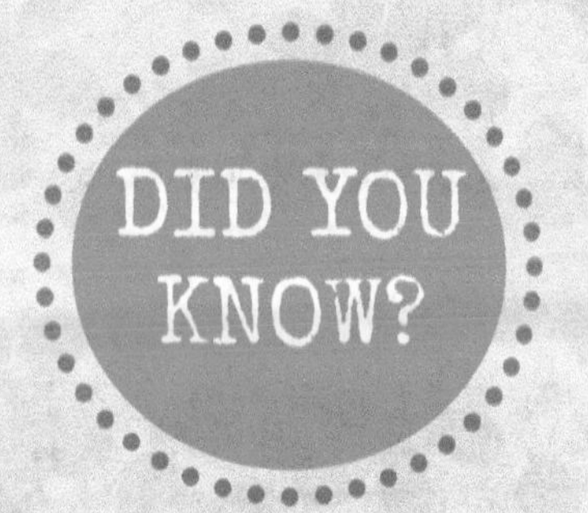

Inhalants

To get high, some kids are breathing in fumes from common household products like hair spray, cleaning fluids, and spray paint. Using inhalants, or "huffing," is EXTREMELY DANGEROUS because these chemicals can make your heart beat irregularly and even make it stop—no matter how young you are. Inhalants can also cause sudden death from suffocating or from choking (usually on vomit). If you are using inhalants, stop now. If you can't stop using them, get help. Talk to your parents or another trusted adult right away. Your life could depend on it!

How should I handle peer pressure to try alcohol, cigarettes, and drugs?

Everybody has heard the words "Just say no!" This is an easy response to any pressure you are feeling to experiment with drugs, alcohol, or cigarettes. The choice to say no and walk away from something is always available to you. You can also talk to your friends about why you have decided not to try drinking or smoking or using drugs. Presenting your reasons will let them know that you mean it when you say no. What you say might also help them make better decisions. You might just "peer pressure" them into *not* smoking or drinking or using drugs—a much healthier choice!

"I'm sure glad I'm not going to get into trouble for being at a party with no adults!"

Pssst! Remember that drinking alcohol at your age is not only dangerous, it's also illegal and using drugs such as marijuana is illegal at any age!

As a general rule, try to avoid situations in which kids might be drinking or doing other risky things. For example, stay away from houses where the parents aren't home and kids are getting together to have a "party." You can always use your parents as an excuse. For example, say "I wish I could go to that party but you know how strict my parents are. I would be grounded forever if I went—it's just not worth it." Your parents won't mind if you use them in this way. In fact, they'll be proud of you!

What if I'm curious about drinking, smoking, or trying drugs?

It's natural to be curious about doing "grown-up" things. You may hear other kids telling stories about trying cigarettes or drinking or experimenting with drugs and you may wonder what it's like.

The reality is that the younger you are when you start smoking or drinking or using drugs, the more likely you are to have a serious problem later. You are more likely to become addicted and experience the harmful effects of these habits on your health. Even at your age, these behaviors can harm your health.

For example, smoking can affect your lungs and reduce your ability to excel in sports, drinking can cloud your judgment and encourage unsafe behaviors, too much alcohol can be fatal, and some drugs such as inhalants can cause sudden death.

If you're considering experimenting with any of these things, first discuss it with your parents or another trusted adult. It's important to think through your decision before you act and to get help understanding the safety issues involved.

You can also do some research on your own about smoking or drinking. The Internet has many sites that will tell you about the dangers of these behaviors. (Go to pages 113 to 115 for some Web sites that provide good information.) If you still want to learn more, ask your health teacher or the school nurse. They can share information about the risks involved in drinking, smoking, and taking drugs.

Why do cliques suddenly seem so important?

A *clique* is a group of friends that behaves exclusively—that is, it excludes, or leaves out, other people. Cliques tend to develop in middle school. Friends in cliques may dress alike and they often have the same taste in music, sports, or other activities. They stick closely together, making it hard for newcomers to join the group.

Many kids your age feel left out of cliques. Kids who are not in cliques sometimes feel that they don't fit well into any of the groups in their school.

Sometimes, kids who are in cliques feel bad, too, because they think they must always act in a certain way. You may feel the need to be in a clique, but keep in mind that cliques can be very limiting. They can prevent you from making a wider variety of friends and experiencing new activities. In other words, involvement in a clique can keep you from growing as a person!

{ **Psst!** No matter what you do, don't worry more about being popular than just being yourself. What makes you awesome is your individuality! }

Why does it seem so important to be popular?

Everybody wants to be liked. It's normal to wonder what other people think of you and to hope they want to be your friends. But remember that not everybody is going to want to be friends with everybody else.

If you are not part of the popular clique, it does not mean that you don't have good friends and are not having lots of fun in and out of school. Concentrate on having friends you feel comfortable talking to and who make you feel good.

CHAPTER NINE:

What About Sex?

An important part of puberty is becoming interested in things having to do with dating and relationships. These issues can be complicated at times. And you may find that you have lots of questions, but are not sure where to go for answers. Your parents and other trusted adults are a good place to start—they'll be able to help and guide you. This chapter can also give you some of the answers you're looking for.

Why do I sometimes feel uncomfortable around boys now?

You probably had both boy and girl friends when you were younger. Now that you are getting older, keeping up your friendships with boys may sometimes feel awkward. Some kids may tease you if you are hanging out with a guy friend, saying that you like him in a romantic way. Or you may be teased for being a tomboy if you choose to hang out with boys.

As you enter puberty, boys may start acting differently around you. They may seem nervous in your company and they might even start to tease you.

There is no good reason why boys and girls should not continue to be good friends. Just as in your friendships with girls, good communication and respect for each other are essential in your friendships with boys.

How will I know when I have a crush on someone?

There are different ways you may discover you are developing a *crush*. Some ways are physical and some are emotional. You might feel nervousness in your stomach, otherwise known as "butterflies." You might feel sweaty or blush whenever the object of your crush is nearby. You might get happy and excited whenever your crush is in the same room.

You might also think about your crush all the time—so much that it may be hard to think about anything else. Your mood may suddenly depend on whether your crush says "hi" to you (you are thrilled) or walks by without seeming to notice you (you are devastated).

Having a crush can be exciting, but it can also be intense. It helps to talk about your feelings with trusted friends and to know that everyone goes through the same thing.

What should I do if I have a crush on a boy?

You can either let him know or you can keep it private. You may decide that your crush is something you want to keep secret. You may have fun just giggling about it with friends. Or you may want to take the risk and let your crush know how you feel. This can be scary—your crush may not feel the same way you do!

Whether or not to reveal your crush is a big decision. You may want to wait until you have a better idea about how *he* feels. Your friends may be able to help you figure this out.

What if I have a crush on another girl?

Having a crush on another girl is okay and normal. Having a crush on a boy or a girl doesn't mean you will always be attracted to people of just that one gender. Figuring out who you are attracted to can be a complicated thing!

You may find that you are interested only in boys, interested only in girls, or somewhere in between. If you feel confused or worried by your feelings, talk to a trusted adult. This could be a parent or someone else in your family, your doctor, or a school counselor.

What if someone has a crush on me but I don't share the same feelings?

That is a tricky situation. Think about how you would want to be treated if you were in the other person's position. You would want to be treated with kindness and respect.

Be as direct and as kind as you can. Let the person know that you don't feel the same way. Don't tell a lot of people about what happened. Imagine how embarrassing this could be for the person who has the crush! After all, no one likes to be rejected.

When are teenagers ready to date?

This is a complicated question with no single correct answer. First, of course, it depends on your family's rules on dating. Some parents feel comfortable with the idea of their children dating in their younger adolescent years (or during middle school), while other parents believe that teenagers need to wait until they are older before dating.

Also think about your own feelings when it comes to dating. Are *you* ready to date? Are you feeling pressure to date before you feel ready? Just because you may have friends who feel ready to date doesn't mean that you are ready.

It's perfectly normal not to feel ready to start dating at your age. There's no rush! You may feel more comfortable developing some non-romantic friendships with boys first. If you *do* feel ready, you may want to think about what your expectations of dating may be. Either way, it's always a good idea to talk with your parents or another trusted adult about this issue.

How can I talk to my parents about dating?

Although it may feel embarrassing to bring up the issue of dating with your parents, it's important to do so. The conversation may be a little awkward at first, but these kinds of conversations get easier the more frequently you have them.

Start by picking a good time for your discussion. Choose a time when you and your parents are both feeling relaxed. Then take a deep breath and say something like "I think I might be ready to start dating. What do you think?" Once the conversation starts, it should continue more easily. But don't be surprised if your parents don't feel that you are ready to date yet. Hear them out and listen to their reasons. Try asking them what age *does* work for them. This is definitely an issue that calls for compromise. (Go back to page 76 for a reminder of how to improve your communication with your parents.)

It's never a good idea to rush into anything until you feel ready and confident that what you are doing is right for you. That way, you won't have regrets later.

How will I know when I'm ready to kiss someone?

Some of your friends may be kissing already. But just because your friends are ready doesn't mean that you are. If you don't feel ready, don't be embarrassed. Many girls your age don't feel comfortable kissing yet and want to wait until they're older.

If you do feel ready for kissing, make sure that it's with someone you trust and feel comfortable with. There should be no pressure on *either* side.

Why is it better to wait until I'm older to think about being sexual with someone?

There are many good reasons for not becoming sexually active until you are older. It is safer—both emotionally and physically—to put this off until you are older. There are lots of responsibilities involved in having sexual contact with another person, and it's important to wait until you feel ready to accept all of these responsibilities. When you have *sex*, you face the possibility of an unplanned pregnancy or getting a sexually transmitted disease (STD; see page 109). And bringing sex into a relationship can make the relationship a lot more complicated and often stressful—especially if one of you is not yet ready to have sex.

There are many ways to feel close with someone without actually having sex. You can still be physically close with someone in ways that feel good but also keep you safe. Holding hands, hugging, kissing, and putting your arm around someone are all healthy ways to show affection. But always remember that no one has a right to touch you anywhere on your body without your permission!

What is sex, anyway?

There are different kinds of sexual activities. Two common ones are sexual intercourse and oral sex. *Sexual intercourse* is when an erect penis enters the vagina. *Oral sex* is when a person uses his or her mouth to stimulate another person's genitals. Anal sex is when an erect penis enters the anus. These are all sexual activities.

Believe it or not, oral sex is really sex. You CAN get STDs, including AIDS, from having oral sex.

When you are older and you make a decision to engage in sexual activity, make sure you know what the responsibilities and risks are. Don't allow anyone to pressure you into doing anything you don't want to do. After all, it's your body and your life—and no one else's.

DID YOU KNOW?

MASTURBATION

Masturbation, or touching your own body, is a normal way to explore your sexual feelings, express the natural sexual response, and safely experiment with sexual touching. Most people of both genders masturbate at least occasionally; others never do. Both are normal. For teenagers, masturbation is a safe way to express and learn more about sexuality without having to worry about pregnancy, having a sexual relationship with another person, or getting a sexually transmitted disease.

DID YOU KNOW?

SEXUAL RESPONSIBILITY

Teens who can talk openly with their parents and who have information about reproduction, sexuality, safer sex, and contraception are more likely to resist peer pressure to have sex and to postpone having sex—and to be responsible when they do become sexually active. Sexual responsibility means making decisions that respect each person's values and goals and promote their self-esteem, not make them feel guilty or ashamed.

What are contraceptives?

Even right before you've started getting periods, having sexual intercourse without a contraceptive can lead to pregnancy. *Contraceptives* are medications or devices that are used to prevent pregnancy, which is why they are often called birth-control methods. There are many different types of contraceptives, including male and female *condoms*, *spermicides*, birth-control pills and patches, and more. When you're ready to learn more about contraceptives, the best places to go for information are your parents or your doctor or other health-care provider.

MYTHBUSTERS

You CAN get pregnant:

* the first time you have sex.
* even if you have sex during your period.
* even if you have sex standing up.
* even if a boy withdraws his penis before ejaculating ("coming").

What are STDs and how do people get them?

You can see why it takes careful planning ahead when you start thinking about becoming sexual with someone. You need to protect yourself from both pregnancy and dangerous infections.

In addition to risking getting pregnant, you can also get infections called *sexually transmitted diseases* (*STDs*) from having sexual intercourse. Some STDs cannot be cured, some can make you unable to have children, and at least one STD can lead to *cancer*. *HIV/AIDS* is an STD that can be fatal.

Of course, the 100-percent most effective way to avoid STDs is to not have sex. When you are ready to have sex, the best way to protect yourself is to always use a condom. Condoms are the only form of birth control that reduces the risk of infection. This is the reason that sex with condoms is often called "safe sex." However, it is really only "safer sex." There is no such thing as perfect protection against STDs other than not having sex. Make sure you know how to use condoms before you have sex for the first time. Find out from a health-care provider—not from a friend, who may not always have reliable information.

When you are sexually active, your doctor will examine you regularly and test you for STDs. Even if you use condoms, it's very important to have regular check-ups to make sure you don't have an STD. Many STDs don't cause any symptoms so you might not realize you have one.

What kinds of touching or sexual behaviors are definitely not okay?

Some forms of sexual behavior, such as those described here, are never okay and always need to be reported immediately and stopped.

Sexual harassment

Sexual harassment is when someone makes unwanted sexual comments or touches you in a sexual way without your permission. Sexual harassment is never acceptable. You have a right to go to school, play on a team, and live in a neighborhood without being harassed.

Some girls report feeling sexually harassed in school. They report that boys make sexual comments to them in the hall or in the lunchroom, that they have had their buttocks or breasts grabbed in the hallways, or that they have heard about sexual comments about specific girls that were written in the boy's bathroom.

If any of these things happen to you, tell someone immediately. Let your parents know what is happening. Tell a teacher, a counselor, or go straight to your school principal. Your school should take this very seriously and needs to make sure that everyone feels safe in the building.

Sexual assault and rape

The law considers any unwanted sexual contact to be *sexual assault.* If you are forced or pressured into having sexual intercourse, it is considered rape. If this happens to you, tell someone immediately. It is never your fault and you have nothing to be embarrassed or ashamed about. Understand that you did not do anything to deserve the assault.

Sexual abuse or molestation

Being touched in a sexual way by an older teen or an adult is *sexual abuse* or *molestation*—even if the person is a relative or friend. It is never okay for an adult to touch a child or a teenager in a sexual way. And it is never the child's fault, even if the child "went along" with the touching. You need to tell your parents or another trusted adult immediately if this happens to you. And keep telling trusted adults until you find someone who will help. You have a right to feel safe.

This relationship stuff is so confusing! I have so many more questions, how do I find the right person to talk to?

It's normal to feel confused when it comes to relationships. You will undoubtedly have lots of questions as you deal with the many complicated issues involved in growing up and becoming an adult. Reading about them is just a starting point. You also need to find knowledgable people you can trust to talk to. You can always talk to your friends, but it's also important to find adults you can talk to as well.

How do you find adults who can help you and who you can trust to keep your conversations confidential? Good people to turn to first are, of course, your parents. Other people you can trust include doctors, nurses, teachers, coaches, school counselors, and grandparents, aunts, uncles, and other older relatives. These trusted adults will be happy to help you with any questions or concerns that you have. Remember: If you keep talking to people, you will find that, over time, relationships will seem a lot less confusing!

NOTE FROM THE AMA

You've reached the end of this book on puberty—but not the end of this exciting and wonderful period in your life! We hope this book has answered many of your questions. Perhaps it has also encouraged you to think of even more questions. Your doctor or other health-care provider is a good person to turn to for answers to your questions, especially if you are uncomfortable talking to other people. Keep in mind that most doctors who treat adolescents provide confidentiality—that is, they will not share information about you or things you have told them with your parents or with anyone else without your permission. Talk to your doctor to find out if he or she provides confidentiality.

Puberty is an exciting, strange, and wonderful process. Some of the changes you go through may seem confusing or challenging at the time. Other changes make your life better and more fulfilling than ever. Try to enjoy this time in your life as much as you can by focusing on all the amazing things you are experiencing and accomplishing on your way to becoming an adult. Good luck!

FIND OUT MORE!

For some more information to help you stay healthy and safe,
check out these Web sites.

BAM! BODY AND MIND

http://www.bam.gov

This site was created by the Centers for Disease Control and Prevention (CDC) to answer teens' questions about everything from physical health to physical education to bullying. It's also a great place to ask a question and get a helpful "Xpert opinion."

CENTER FOR YOUNG WOMEN'S HEALTH

http://www.youngwomenshealth.org

This helpful site is offered by the Center for Young Women's Health at Children's Hospital Boston. The site provides lots of information on a wide variety of topics—from nutrition basics, to safety on the Internet, to depression and eating disorders. The information is presented in friendly, easy-to-understand language.

4 GIRLS HEALTH

http://www.4girls.gov

Developed by the Office on Women's Health in the Department of Health and Human Services, this site gives girls between the ages of 10 and 16 reliable, up-to-date health information. The site focuses on general health issues, providing positive, supportive messages to encourage healthful behaviors in girls and young women.

FOR KIDS ONLY

http://www.health.org/features/kidsarea/kidsarea.aspx

This site offers usable information in a kid-friendly way to help kids understand the dangers of drinking alcohol and using drugs. Lots of helpful tips on what to do if you or a friend is drinking or using drugs.

GIRL POWER

http://www.girlpower.gov

Sponsored by the U.S. Department of Health and Human Services, this Web site addresses girls ages 9 to 13. While the site's emphasis is on health and safety issues, it also offers several interactive features, like games, puzzles, and instructions for craft activities.

KIDS HEALTH

http://www.kidshealth.org

This Web site targets many different audiences. It provides extensive information to kids, including tips for staying healthy; avoiding alcohol, drugs, and cigarettes; a glossary of medical terms; and much, much more. Adults can obtain practical parenting information and keep up with recent news articles about health issues.

NATIONAL ASSOCIATION OF ANOREXIA AND ASSOCIATED DISORDERS

http://www.anad.org

This is an excellent resource for people who have an eating disorder or who know someone who has an eating disorder. It offers information about eating disorders and treatment centers that specialize in eating disorders. Message boards, chat rooms, and important hotline information are also available.

NATIONAL COALITION FOR GAY, LESBIAN, AND BISEXUAL AND TRANSGENDER YOUTH

http://www.outproud.org

Provides information and resources for gay, lesbian, bisexual, and transgender teens as well as for their family and friends. What is going on in schools today? Who are your community role models? Who are your peers, and how do they feel? Get answers to these questions and more at this site.

SAFE YOUTH/NATIONAL VIOLENCE PREVENTION RESOURCE CENTER

http://www.safeyouth.org

This is a one-stop shop for information on preventing youth violence, from bullying to teen dating violence to gang activity. The site lots of links to other helpful sites.

SOY UNICA

http://www.soyunica.gov/present/

This site is for teen girls who want information on issues related to adolescence from a Latina perspective. The site provides information in both English and Spanish. This site can help you learn about your body, plan for your future, take part in a poll, or just get to know yourself better!

STOP BULLYING NOW/HEALTH RESOURCES AND SERVICES ADMINISTRATION

http://stopbullyingnow.hrsa.gov/index.asp?area=main

This government-sponsored Web site offers lots of fun, interactive games to help kids understand what bullying is and how to prevent it or stop it. The information is for kids who are being bullied, who witness bullying, or who bully other kids. It also provides information to adults about what they can do to help.

TALKING WITH KIDS

http://www.talkingwithkids.org

This Web site is aimed at parents, providing helpful information about how to communicate with their kids about tough issues such as sex, violence, drugs, and alcohol. Although directed primarily at parents, kids can also benefit from the information.

TIPS 4 YOUTH/CENTERS FOR DISEASE CONTROL AND PREVENTION/ TIPS 4 YOUTH

http://www.cdc.gov/tobacco/tips4youth.htm

This government-sponsored Web site provides kids with lots of information about the dangers of smoking as well as motivation and tips for quitting. It has colorful posters and interactive animated features that appeal to kids.

GLOSSARY

This glossary defines some common terms you will find in this book. Words in italics are defined elsewhere in the glossary

acanthosis nigricans – raised, velvety, darkened patches on the skin on the back of the neck, armpits, and groin that make the skin look dirty, occurring most often in young people who are overweight

acne – a skin condition that causes *blackheads*, *whiteheads*, and/or *pimples*

AIDS – acquired immunodeficiency syndrome, the most advanced stages of *infection* with *HIV*

antibiotic – a type of medicine used to treat *infections* caused by *bacteria*

antiperspirant – a product used to prevent perspiration or sweating

anus – the opening from which solid waste leaves the body

areola – the circle of darker-colored skin around the *nipple*

bacteria – microscopic organisms that can sometimes cause *infection*

benzoyl peroxide – a medication used to help fight *acne*

blackhead – a *blemish* that develops when a clogged *hair follicle* is exposed to air (referred to medically as an open comedone)

blemish – an imperfection, mark, or flaw; a *pimple* is a blemish on the skin

breast bud – a small round bump of breast tissue underneath the *nipple*; an early sign of *puberty* in girls

bully – a person who tries to make another person feel bad

calcium – an important *mineral* used by the body to build bones and teeth

calorie – a unit of energy the body gets from food

cancer – a disease in which abnormal cells in the body multiply and destroy healthy tissue

cervix – the bottom portion of the *uterus* that has an opening into the *vagina*

clique – a group of friends that excludes other people

clitoris – a pea-sized mound of tissue above the *urinary opening* that responds with sexual sensations when stimulated

condom – a thin rubber or plastic covering worn on an erect penis (male condom) or inserted into the *vagina* (female condom) before *sex* to help prevent pregnancy and *sexually transmitted diseases*

contraceptive – a medication or device used to prevent pregnancy

cramp – a painful contraction of one or more muscles; contractions of the *uterus* can cause cramps during *periods*

crush – a strong feeling of attraction to another person

deodorant – a product that prevents or covers up unwanted odor

dermatologist – a doctor who treats skin problems

dietitian – a person who has completed a degree in nutrition and has also passed the dietitian exam; teaches people how to eat healthfully

discharge – fluid that is released from the body

duct – a tube in the body that carries liquid or air

eczema – red, itchy patches on the skin that sometimes join together, occurring most often on the inner part of the elbows or behind the knees

electrolysis – the destruction of hair roots using an electric current

endometrium – the lining of the *uterus* that is made up of blood and tissue that is expelled from the body during *menstruation*

fallopian tubes – the two tubes that stretch from the *ovaries* to the *uterus*; the ovaries release mature eggs into the fallopian tubes

follicultis – raised bumps on the skin brought on through shaving

genitals – the reproductive *organs*, especially referring to those outside the body

gland – an *organ* in the body that produces a substance (a *hormone*) to be used elsewhere in the body

hair follicle – an opening in the skin through which hair grows

heredity – the passing on of qualities and traits from one generation to the next through genetic material

HIV – human immunodeficiency syndrome, the virus that causes *AIDS*; HIV is transmitted through contact with infected blood or other body fluids, usually by having unprotected *sex* with an infected person or by sharing contaminated needles

hormone – a chemical substance that controls one or more body functions

hydrogen peroxide – a chemical used in bleaches or hair dyes to bleach or color hair; also used in tooth-bleaching products; also used in or as a disinfectant to kill germs

hymen – a thin layer of tissue at the opening of the *vagina*

infection – invasion and multiplication of germs such as viruses or *bacteria* in the body; an infection can occur in one part of the body or spread throughout the body

inflammation – the body's response to a local *infection*, characterized by redness, heat, swelling, and pain

keloid – an abnormal, raised, hard scar that grows in an area of skin damage; some people can develop keloids after body piercings or tattoos

labia, majora and minora – the outer and inner "lips" around the opening into the *vagina*

lubricate – to make smooth or slippery

masturbation – stimulation of one's own *genitals* for sexual pleasure

menstrual cycle – the length of time from the first day of a menstrual period to the first day of the next period

menstruation – a discharge of blood and tissue from the *uterus*, usually occurring about once a month

mineral – chemicals found in foods and elsewhere; some minerals are essential for healthy functioning of the body

moles – round or oval spots on the skin that are usually dark brown and can be flat or raised

molestation – unwanted sexual touching of one person by another

mons – a small, rounded pad of fat that lies over the pubic bone

nipple – the tip of the breast that projects out; milk flows out of the body through the nipples during breast-feeding non-comedogenic – does not clog pores; skin products with "non-comedogenic" on the label do not contribute to the development of *acne*

nutrient – a substance required by living things to live and grow

oral sex – a type of sexual activity in which a person uses his or her mouth to stimulate another person's *genitals*

organ – a part of an animal or plant that performs one or more specific functions

ovaries – the pair of organs that stores and regularly releases eggs

ovulation – the release of a mature egg from an *ovary*

peer pressure – pressure from one's acquaintances, or peers, to behave in a certain way

pelvis – a ring of bones in the lower abdominal area that protects the pelvic *organs* such as the *uterus*, *ovaries*, and bladder

period – the common name for *menstruation*

pimples – small areas of *inflammation* on the skin that are filled with *pus*

PMS – premenstrual syndrome, the time before a *period* during which a woman's *hormones* can fluctuate and affect her mood and cause physical symptoms

proteins – chemicals that form the structure of plants and animals; proteins in foods are essential for the body's proper growth, development, and functioning

psoriasis – patches of thick, raised skin that are pink or red and covered with silverish white scales, occurring most often on the knees, elbows, and scalp

puberty – the time during which the body grows from that of a child to that of an adult; the time during which the reproductive system matures

pubic hair – hair that grows in the genital area

pus – a creamy fluid produced as the body fights an *infection*

salicylic acid – a mild acid in some medicines used to treat *acne*; it stimulates peeling of the top layer of skin and opens plugged *hair follicles*

sanitary pad – a pad made of absorbent material placed in the underpants during a *period* to absorb menstrual blood

scoliosis – a condition in which the spine curves to the left or right

sebum – an oily substance including some skin debris that makes the skin smooth but can also clog *hair follicles* and cause *acne*

sex – a general term to describe sexual activities such as vaginal intercourse, *oral sex*, or anal sex

sexual abuse of a child – sexual mistreatment of a child, including sexual contact between an older teen or an adult and a child

sexual assault – any type of forced or unwanted sexual contact

sexual harassment – any repeated, unwanted behavior of a sexual nature performed by one person against another

sperm – the male cell of reproduction

spermicide – a substance that kills *sperm,* used to prevent pregnancy

SPF – sun protection factor, a rating used on skin-care products to indicate the product's level of protection against sunburn

sterile – free of dirt or germs

steroids – *hormones* the body produces to help the body deal with stress and to promote growth and development

STD – sexually transmitted disease, an *infection* transmitted by sexual activity

stretch mark – a purple or white line that can appear on the skin when, for example, a person grows quickly

tampon – a plug of cotton or other absorbent material that is inserted into the *vagina* during a *period* to absorb menstrual blood

toxic shock syndrome – a rare but serious *infection* caused by *bacteria,* occurring mostly among menstruating women who use *tampons*

urinary opening – the opening through which urine leaves the body

uterus – a hollow, muscular *organ* in a woman's *pelvis* that has a lining that sheds during each *period;* the *organ* in which a fetus develops during pregnancy

vagina – a muscular tube that leads from the external *genitals* to the *uterus;* a baby passes through the vagina during delivery

vaginal opening – the opening into the *vagina*

vegetarian – a person who does not eat meat, poultry, or fish, and sometimes also avoids all animal products such as eggs and milk

vigorous – full of physical strength

vitamins – nutrients found in foods that are essential to good health

vulva – the outer, visible female genital area

warts – hard lumps with a rough surface that are caused by a virus, occurring most often on the arms, legs, hands, and face; plantar warts develop on the bottoms of the feet; genital warts are an *STD*

whitehead – a white *blemish* on the skin that develops when a *hair follicle* is clogged and covered and not exposed to air (referred to medically as a closed comedone)

INDEX

A

Acanthosis nigricans, 38
Acne, 33-36
Aerobic(s), 18,19
AIDS, 107, 109
Alcohol, 93, 96-98
Aluminum (in antiperspirants), 40
Anal sex, 107
Anger, 77, 78
Anorexia nervosa, 22
Antibiotic, 36
Antiperspirant, 40
Anus, 60
Areola, 54

B

Bacteria, 33-36, 39
Benzoyl peroxide, 35, 36
Blackhead(s), 33-34
Blemish(es), 33-38
Body odor, 39
Body hair, 46-49
Bra, 10, 56-58
Bra size guide, 57
Breast(s), 50-59, 67
Breast bud(s), 52
Breast development (stages), 52
Breast exam(s), 55
Bulimia nervosa, 22
Bully(ing), 91, 92

C

Caffeine, 82
Calcium, 16, 30, 31
Calorie(s), 15, 16, 21
Cancer, 109
Cervix, 61, 62
Cigarettes, 93, 96-98
Clique(s), 98, 99
Clitoris, 60
Communication, 75-76
Compromise, 76
Condom(s), 108, 109
Contraceptive(s), 108, 109
Cramp(s), 71
Crush(es), 101-103

D

Dating, 100, 103-105
Death/dying, 84
Dental care, 42
Deodorant, 40, 63
Depression, 83
Dermatologist, 36
Dietitian, 17
Discharge, 55, 62
Divorce, 84-85
Douche, 63
Drinking, 93, 96-98
Drugs, 93, 96-98
Duct(s), 51

E

Eating disorder(s), 22
Eczema, 38
Egg(s) (in ovaries), 61, 64, 65
Ejaculation, 108
Electrolysis, 49
Endometrium, 64, 65
Estrogen, 61
Exercise, 14-23

F

Fallopian tubes, 61
Fashion models, 11
Feminine hygiene spray, 63
Fertilization, 65
Fetus, 62
Fight(s), 88
Flexibility, 18, 19
Follicle(s), 33
Folliculitis, 48
Food pyramid, 16
Foot odor, 40
Friendship, 87-94

G

Genital(s), 46, 59, 60
Gland(s), 39
Grief, 84
Growth spurt, 27

H

Hair care, 43-45
Hair follicle(s), 33
Harassment, 59, 110
Height, 26-29
Heredity, 19, 29, 44
Hormone(s), 10, 33-35, 61, 71, 73
Huffing, 96
Hydrogen peroxide, 42
Hymen, 60, 68

I

Infection(s), 41, 109
Inflammation, 33
Inhalants, 96
Intercourse, 60, 68, 107-109

K

Keloids, 41
Kissing, 105, 106

L

Labia, 60
Lubricate, 32

M

Makeup, 35
Masturbation, 63, 107
Menstrual blood, 64-70
Menstrual cycle, 35, 55, 62, 64-71
Menstrual cycle (chart), 65
Menstrual period(s), 7, 21, 29, 64-71
Milk ducts, 51
Milk glands, 51
Mineral(s), 17
Moisturizer, 35
Mole(s), 38
Molestation, 110
Mons, 60

N

Negotiating, 76
Nipple(s), 52, 54, 55,
Non-comedogenic, 35, 36
Nutrient(s), 17

O

Oral sex, 107
Organ(s), 59-62
Ova (eggs in ovaries), 61
Ovaries, 61, 64-65
Overeating (compulsive), 22
Ovulation, 65, 66

P

Peer pressure, 93-97
Pelvis, 62

Period(s), 7, 21, 64-71
Perspiration, 39
Piercing, 41
Pimple(s), 33-36
PMS (premenstrual syndrome), 70
Popularity, 99
Prioritizing, 76
Pregnancy, 62, 106, 107, 108
Protein(s), 17
Psoriasis, 38
Puberty, 6-11, 26, 27, 34, 39, 43, 46, 54, 55, 61, 67, 75, 90, 100
Pubic hair, 46, 47
Pubic hair growth (stages), 47
Pus, 33

R

Rape, 110
Relationship(s), 10, 86-99, 100, 111

S

Salicylic acid, 36
Sanitary pad(s), 68, 69, 70
Scoliosis, 31
Sebum, 32
Separation, 84
Sex, 100-111
Sexual abuse, 110
Sexual assault, 110
Sexual harassment, 59, 110
Shoplifting, 93, 94
Shyness, 79
Smoking, 93, 96-98
Sperm, 64
Spermicides, 108
SPF (sun protection factor), 36, 37
STD (sexually transmitted disease), 106, 107, 109
Sterile, 41
Steroids, 33
Strengthening exercise(s), 18, 19
Stress, 35, 72, 82, 83
Stretch marks, 39, 54
Sunscreen, 36, 37
Sweat, 39, 40

T

Tampon(s), 68, 69, 70
Tattoo(s), 41
Teeth, 42
Testosterone, 61

U

Urinary opening, 60
Uterus, 61, 62, 65

V

Vagina, 61, 62, 68
Vaginal opening, 60
Vegetarian(s), 17, 24
Vitamin(s), 17
Vulva, 60

W

Wart(s), 38
Waxing, 48, 49
Web sites, 113-115
Weight, 14-23
Whitehead(s), 33, 34
Wrinkles, 36

MEET THE MEDICAL EDITOR

Amy B. Middleman, MD, MSEd, MPH, is a board-certified Adolescent Medicine specialist and Associate Professor of Pediatrics at Baylor College of Medicine in Houston. She is a practicing physician specializing in the care of adolescents at Texas Children's Hospital. Dr. Middleman is the Adolescent Medicine editor for the medical online text UpToDate and serves as the Society for Adolescent Medicine's liaison member of the Advisory Committee on Immunization Practices with the Centers for Disease Control and Prevention (CDC) in Atlanta. In addition to her Doctor of Medicine degree, she has a Master of Science in Education and a Master of Public Health degree.

MEET THE WRITER

Kate Gruenwald Pfeifer, LCSW, is a licensed clinical social worker. She has a Masters degree in social work from Columbia University as well as a certificate in psychodynamic psychotherapy with children and adolescents from NYU Psychoanalytic Institute. Pfeifer, whose practice specializing in children and adolescents is in Millburn, New Jersey, is a school social worker and supervisor of several middle school social work programs. She is also the writer of the *American Medical Association's Boy's Guide to Becoming a Teen*.